P9-DYD-974

LEADERSHIP IN TRANSITION

LEADERSHIP IN TRANSITION

The Community College Presidency

George B. Vaughan
George Mason University

AMERICAN COUNCIL ON EDUCATION
MACMILLAN PUBLISHING COMPANY
New York
Collier Macmillan Publishers
London

Macmillan Publishing Company
866 Third Avenue, New York, N.Y. 10022

Collier Macmillan Canada, Inc.

Library of Congress Catalog Card Number: 89–6575

Printed in the United States of America

printing number

1   2   3   4   5   6   7   8   9   10

Library of Congress Cataloging-in-Publication Data

Vaughan, George B.
  Leadership in transition : the community college presidency /
George B. Vaughan.
     p.   cm.
  Bibliography: p.
  Includes index.
  ISBN 0–02–897441–7
  1. Community colleges—United States—Administration.
2. Community college presidents—United States.   I. Title.
LB2341.V346 1989
378.1'11—dc20   89–6575
                                                                                 CIP

To the faculty, staff, and board
of Piedmont Virginia Community College,
without whose cooperation and inspiration I
could not have completed this book

CONTENTS

Foreword by Johnas F. (Jeff) Hockaday   ix

Preface   xi

Acknowledgments   xiii

1   Leaders in Search of a Focus   1

2   The President as Educational Leader   17

3   The Mystique of the Presidency   32

4   How Long Is Too Long? The Question Presidents and
    Trustees Fear to Ask   46

Introduction to Chapters Five and Six   65

5   Women Who Are Presidents   69

6   The Minority Presidents   87

7   The Next Generation   109

8   Advice for Those Who Would Be President   125

Bibliography   141

Index   145

FOREWORD

Persons interested in the past, present, and future of community college leadership will find *Leadership In Transition: The Community College Presidency* to be an exciting and informative book, written by one of America's foremost writers on community colleges. In an earlier book, *The Community College Presidency*, George Vaughan researched the social and economic backgrounds, as well as the preparation and values, of those who become presidents of community and junior colleges. In this book he moves onward to study leadership rather than leaders, and to examine how leadership is and should be changing. Dr. Vaughan's premise is that the formative years of community college development have largely passed and that leadership must change to meet the needs of a new era, an era as exciting as its predecessor but in a different manner. Vaughan expresses concern for the new leadership: what kind of leadership will it be, and what kind of leaders are available to meet this change?

This book provides material for reflection and reaction from those of us who worked during the formative years of community college development and who will work in these colleges in the future. This book is needed by those who will be the presidents in the new era—those who never knew the excitement of the building years but who will know the excitement of refinement, of changing techniques and technologies, and of colleges that serve publics different from those of the 1970s and 1980s. Thus, this book will be a valuable blueprint for future leaders, and could well become the classic text for that purpose.

The first two chapters provide a solid foundation for a book on changing leadership. Chapter 1 gives valuable insight into what the future may need in leadership: what will its focus be? Chapter 2 speaks of the presidents and educational leadership. Specifically, it gives insight on what educational leadership is and, equally important, on what it is not.

Chapter 4 is must reading for incumbent presidents and boards of trustees. The question of "How Long Is Too Long?" in reference to the tenure of a president is an intense question that must be answered, and it must be answered by all of us. This chapter gives wonderful advice on those things that must be considered. I especially like the thrust that is given to the role of trustees in the matter of tenure for a president. Chapter 4 is the best work I have read on this very important subject—a masterpiece!

The chapters on women and minority presidents are insightful works on how women and minorities feel about the presidency. There are some surprises here. Look carefully at what these two groups of presidents have to say.

The findings in Chapter 7 are unexpected. Dr. Vaughan compares those who will be presidents in the future with those who are presidents now or were presidents in the recent past. The differences in social and economic backgrounds and in academic preparation destroyed my notions of what they were to be. This is a very interesting chapter.

My favorite part of the book is Chapter 8. Here is George Vaughan at his very best. This chapter comes from the heart, the head, and the intuitions of an outstanding community college president. This is must reading for anyone who aspires to the presidency of a community or junior college. It is Dr. Vaughan's most significant gift to this profession—outstanding!

George Vaughan has served as the president of two community colleges in Virginia; in both instances with distinction. At the present time, he is director of the Community College Leadership Program at George Mason University. From that vantage point, he will influence many future leaders of community colleges in America. This book, *Leadership in Transition: The Community College Presidency,* will become a landmark publication in his quest to provide that influence, as leadership moves from the past to the future. I recommend it highly to all who will have a share of the future.

Jeff Hockaday
Chancellor,
Virginia Community College System

PREFACE

In 1986, I wrote and the American Council on Education and Macmillan published *The Community College Presidency*. The following is from the preface to the 1986 volume:

> As the first major publication about the community college presidency, this book is devoted to providing an understanding of an important but often neglected subject. Most presidents, trustees, would-be presidents, faculty members, scholars of higher education, and others interested in the community college have little or no knowledge about who has led these institutions, who is leading them now, and, perhaps more significant, who will lead them in the future. This volume is a major step toward filling that void.

The current volume picks up where the 1986 volume left off. For example, the 1986 volume discussed the concept of burnout and concluded that most presidents are not burned out. The current volume goes beyond burnout in its interpretation and asks a more relevant question: "How long is too long for a president to serve while continuing to provide effective leadership?"

The 1986 volume speculated about who would be leading the nation's community colleges in the future. The current volume documents who the future presidents will likely be.

As in the previous volume, the current volume uses quotes as well as statistics to interpret the community college presidency. A brief overview of the chapters included in the current volume follows.

Chapter 1 briefly describes the role of those who served as the founding presidents of community colleges during the 1960s and early 1970s. The thesis of the chapter is that the founding presidents had a focus for their presidency—to construct buildings, to employ faculty and staff, and to enroll students—but that the current community college presidency suffers from a lack of focus. Suggestions are made for bringing focus to the presidency.

Chapter 2 discusses the role of the president as educational leader. It concludes that, to be effective, the president must be the college's educational leader.

Chapter 3 is likely to be somewhat controversial among presidents and trustees. Entitled "The Mystique of the Presidency," the chapter presents the belief that community college presidents, by speaking on everything, are heard on nothing. The chapter suggests that presidents place greater distance between themselves and their various constituents.

Chapter 4 asks and answers the question "How long is too long to remain in a given presidency?" While there is no set number of years for effective leadership, certain signs indicate when presidents have stayed too long.

Chapter 5 discusses female presidents. What are the special problems they face in seeking the presidency? Are there advantages to being a female president? And what social forces have influenced women in their move into the presidency?

Chapter 6 discusses black and Hispanic community college presidents. Questions similar to those asked of female presidents were asked of blacks and Hispanics. The answers, however, are often different from those provided by women.

Chapter 7 examines those who currently serve as deans of instruction in the nation's community colleges. Deans of instruction are important to the future of the community college, and if history is any indicator, they will be very prominent among the next generation of presidents. Based upon a major national survey, the answers to who will make up the next generation of presidents offer some surprises.

Chapter 8, based upon interviews and observations of the author, offers practical advice for those who make the community college presidency their career goal. The potential president is provided with many "dos and don'ts" in seeking the office.

To summarize, this volume brings focus to the presidency not only for presidents but also for trustees, faculty members, future presidents, and scholars interested in understanding this important question.

ACKNOWLEDGMENTS

This book is dedicated to the faculty, staff, and board of Piedmont Virginia Community College. While the entire college community contributed to the environment that made it possible for me to work on the book, certain individuals were especially helpful and kind toward me during the time I was doing the work. Therefore, I wish to offer additional thanks to the following: Jan Kessler for her encouragement and assistance; Linda Ragland for always being concerned and helping in any way she could; Barbara McCauley for serving as a one-person cheering squad; and to Pat Buck, for her sensitivity, intelligence, interest, professional skills, and friendship. Board members Elizabeth Woodard and James Batten were always encouraging and were especially so during the periods of my annual evaluations.

In addition to the above members of the college community, Ronald Head helped me develop the surveys and interpret the results. And I will always be indebted to James Perkins for the careful and critical reading he did of the entire manuscript. His scholarship and friendly advice contributed greatly to the finished product.

Jennings Wagoner was invaluable in his critique of the manuscript. He embodies the concept of the gentleman and the scholar. I will always appreciate the time he took from an extremely busy schedule to offer me many suggestions for improving the manuscript.

Robert Templin's comments on chapter 2, The President as Educational Leader, helped bring focus to the chapter. Richard Richardson's comments were equally helpful on the chapters dealing with female and minority presidents. Beth Haury improved the style and wording of the entire manuscript. Don Puyear's help in analyzing the survey data was helpful, as was Evelyn House's coding of the information.

James Murray has been and continues to be a source of inspiration, information, and friendship. No author has ever been more fortunate than I to work closely with someone of Jim's knowledge, talents, and caring. Lloyd Chilton also provided his steady influence and was always available in my many times of need. His associates at Macmillan were equally willing to help. The copy editor was excellent, preserving the integrity of the author while at the same time improving the manuscript considerably.

Since assuming my present position, I have been fortunate to profit from the friendship and professional assistance of Kathleen McGuinness and Brenda Noel. They have provided the moral support I had to have during my transitional period. Also, the many kindnesses shown to me by Wade Gilley and James Fonseca helped make it possible for me to finish the book.

Jeff Hockaday, my boss during the time most of the work was done on the book, has always encouraged me to write and has always helped me in disseminating my work. Had his attitude been otherwise, it is likely that I would not have been able to continue to write while I was a president.

I am deeply indebted to all of the deans and presidents who returned my surveys. Without their responses, the book could not have been written. The same is true of the board members and presidents who consented to be interviewed. The wisdom contained in the volume comes from the participants in the work.

David Riesman commented on earlier versions of the pages dealing with scholarship and the role of the president in "balancing the presidential seesaw." His wisdom is amazing and his willingness to help unselfish. Marian Gade was helpful in her review of the chapter on the president as educational leader.

Finally, Peggy was her usual self: unselfish, critical in the best possible sense of the term, encouraging, and unrelenting in her demand that the book be the best one I could possibly write. During the years I have been writing, she has truly been my mentor, and to her I owe much of whatever successes I might have enjoyed over the years. Brandt and Andrew have continued to support me and to give up time with me when necessary in order that I could complete the project at hand. Without the support of Peggy, Brandt, and Andrew, my work would be much less enjoyable and much less productive.

1

LEADERS IN SEARCH OF A FOCUS

A President either is constantly on top of events, or, if he hesitates, events will soon be on top of him.

    —Harry S Truman

Little wonder that community college watchers are often at a loss to fathom the educational undertaking when even those closest to its heartbeat are often perplexed when attempting to explain it. Like the mythical sea-god Proteus, once you have it in your grasp, it is likely to present an entirely different form.

    —Peggy A. Vaughan

He was still the Captain, but no one had seemed to notice that there was no troop and no war. . . . He had been in charge so long that everyone assumed all thoughts, questions, needs and wants had to be referred to him, however simple these might be. It was ingrained in him, he had done it so long, but he was aware that it wasn't appropriate anymore.

    —Larry McMurtry, *Lonesome Dove*

During the boom period of public community college growth,[1] community college presidents came from backgrounds as varied as the colleges they led. In contrast to the fact that almost 90 percent of today's presidents

[1]According to the American Association of Community and Junior Colleges (supplement to the AACJC *Letter,* no. 234, March 24, 1987) over 650 public two-year institutions were founded from 1957 to 1977; enrollment in these colleges grew from 776, 493 in 1957 to almost 4 million in 1977.

came to the presidency from within the community college ranks, almost one-fourth of the presidents in 1960 came from public school administration and over 15 percent came from four-year institutions. Other presidents came from branch colleges, from technical schools, and in some cases directly from graduate schools, as well as from within the community college ranks (Vaughan 1986, pp. 28–31). The founding presidents opened new colleges, a herculean task they performed extremely well. Moreover, these presidents played a major role in shaping the community college's mission and the image of the presidency.

In the formative years of community college development, colleges were opened in storefronts, in army barracks, and on abandoned chicken farms. Those were the years before community-based and lifelong learning became a part of the community college's lexicon. Those were the years before governing boards understood what a community college could and should be, years when they called Edmund J. Gleazer, Jr., chief executive officer of the American Association of Junior Colleges, to tell him that "they wanted to open a community college but knew nothing about them. They wanted somebody who knew something about them. So there was an expertise they were looking for at the time; the president was supposed to know, beyond anyone else, what the institution was supposed to be" (quoted in ibid., p. 89).

During the 1960s and 1970s, which were tremendously important years for the community college in the United States, the community college philosophy and, in many respects, the image of the presidency were shaped. The founding presidents were active individuals with little time for reflection. Riding the crest of a movement that took all their time and energy, they had little of either to devote to the future, to reflection; every minute of every day was devoted to building colleges and selling the mission to legislators, the faculty, and the public, often simultaneously. While few presidents thought about the future, they knew what the institution was supposed to be *at that point in time;* they knew that the community college was democracy's answer to the call for universal higher education, to opening the door of opportunity to everyone. Thus also knew what their own role was at that point; they realized that most mistakes in management would be forgiven or ignored as long as enrollments increased, campuses grew, and the public applauded. Although the founding presidents were often autocratic individuals and poor managers who generally promised more than they could deliver and embraced the community college mission as an act of faith rather than through some well-thought-out process, they had a focus for the office they occupied. They focused on a vision born of faith, shaped in the present, and grounded in the belief that higher education was the main avenue for curing many of society's ills, including poverty and its progeny, ignorance. The centerpiece of their vision was the open-access, comprehensive public community college. The founding presidents spent hours, days, and

even years communicating their vision of the community college to anyone who would listen, and literally millions of people not only listened
but heeded their message and supported these institutions by attending
them and by contributing financial support.

LEADERS ON THE EDGE

To understand the founding community college presidents, one must be
aware that they were on the leading edge of a movement involving a large
segment of society, a movement that promised sweeping educational and
social changes, a movement that, like all broad-based movements, had
implications for the future. John Gardner's observations about the nation's founding fathers may help in understanding the role of the founding
community college presidents.

Speaking of the great political leaders of eighteenth-century America,
Gardner writes: "The sense of history surrounding the events of the day
was intense, the need for leadership urgent and compelling." He continues, "The leaders had been handed a shaping role in history and they
knew it. In the creation of the new nation, the clay was awaiting the hand
of the potter. It was a challenge well suited to stimulate and develop leadership." Gardner paints the early leaders as optimists who "believed that
the locus of responsibility was in them and saw themselves as shapers of
the future. And they shared a set of values and philosophical views. . . ."
(Gardner 1987, no. 6, p. 4). Although the achievements and lasting influence of the nation's early political leaders were on a different plane from
that of the early community college presidents, the parallels are similar
in kind if not in degree and thereby provide a valuable perspective for
viewing those community college presidents who either founded colleges
or served as presidents during the period of rapid enrollment growth. Indeed, most community college presidents who functioned during the
1960s and early 1970s can readily identify with Gardner's description of
the nation's early leaders.

Many early community college presidents, while accepting their roles
without question, sensed that the moment was right for taking higher education to the masses; most early community college presidents realized
that, as "doers and builders," their job was to provide colleges that were
accessible, both physically and philosophically, to almost everyone.
Caught up in the wave of excitement and energy that engulfs those in the
vanguard of great societal movements, few of the early presidents paused
to contemplate what they or their successors would do as leaders once
the growth period ended; few of the early leaders made any attempt to
interpret what the community college meant to the broader aspects of
society. Their philosophy was America's philosophy: bigger (larger and
more colleges with more and more students) was better. Their philosophy

was rooted in America's political and social philosophy: opportunity for everyone and more education for more people was not only desirable but an American mandate.[2]

Although most presidents devoted little time to examining their own role other than as it related to achieving the objectives at hand, and although very few community college leaders attempted to examine the community college's role in relationship to the broader movements within society, there nevertheless emerged a feeling of manifest destiny on the part of the presidents and those faculty members and trustees who looked to them for leadership. The early presidents knew, almost by instinct it seemed at times, the role the community college *must* play if the nation were to keep its promise of equal opportunity for minorities, women, the economically and socially disadvantaged, the academically weak, and others in American society who seemed destined to linger forever on the periphery of the American dream.

Did the founding community college presidents have a sense of history, a sense of being a part of something bigger than themselves? Most probably they did not, for it is only the true visionaries, the leaders of leaders, who fully grasp the implications of what is happening around them. In Gardner's discussion of the nation's early political leaders, he notes that although many people shared the beliefs of the leaders of early eighteenth-century America, "Only a few left their names in the history books" (Gardner 1987, no. 6, p. 5). A few of the early community college presidents must have sensed that they were on the leading edge of a new era in higher education.

If a comprehensive history of the community college movement in the United States is ever written, certain presidents will leave their names in the history books, for never before (or since) has any nation committed itself to universal higher education; never before or since have so many individuals had the opportunity to found colleges. The idea of open access to higher education was a powerful force working with any number of ideas and actions to provide the philosophical base for the founding community college presidents in much the same way that the ideas of freedom and democracy united the nation's early leaders. Just as late eighteenth-century America provided the perfect setting for Jefferson, Madison, and

---

[2]Noteworthy exceptions to this statement were Clyde E. Blocker and Richard C. Richardson, Jr., who, along with Robert H. Plummer, wrote *The Two-Year College: A Social Synthesis* in 1965. While the volume did not deal with the presidency as such, it is nevertheless an important statement on the development and role of the community college in America. At the time the volume was published, both Blocker and Richardson were community college presidents. Other individuals devoted much time and energy to interpreting what the community college could and should be, although almost no discussion was devoted to the community college presidency. The person who did the most to shape the community college mission during the boom years was Edmund J. Gleazer, Jr., president of the American Association of Community and Junior Colleges from April 1, 1958, until June 30, 1981.

others to put their ideas into action, the 1960s provided the perfect setting for community colleges and their leaders to preach their cause and to promote the democratization of higher education.

While one can view the activities of the nation's early leaders only through the eyes of historians, the founding community college presidents are much closer to us, with a dwindling number continuing to serve as presidents today. Since the position of community college president is a relatively new one, a more contemporary analogy might serve to help us to understand the founding presidents' role. In many respects, the early community college presidents epitomized the type of business leader Michael Maccoby refers to as the "gamesman." Maccoby believes that after the 1950s the gamesman emerged to meet the needs of the modern organization. His gamesman is competitive, innovative, independent, fast-moving, and flexible.

> The modern gamesman is best defined as a person who loves change and
> wants to influence its course. He likes to take calculated risks and is
> fascinated by technique and new methods. He sees a developing project,
> human relations, and his own career in terms of options and possibilities, as
> if they were a game. . . . [He is] fair and unprejudiced but contemptuous of
> weakness; tough and dominating but not destructive." (Maccoby 1976, p. 100)

Maccoby adds: "More than any other types, gamesmen told us that the ability to dramatize ideas and to stimulate or activate others were *[sic]* among the most important abilities for their work" (ibid., p. 104).

But even successful gamesmen developed some problems. Maccoby's gamesmen played to win and derived their pleasure from the contest: new plays, new options, and control of the situation (ibid., p. 105). However,

> The typical gamesman's mid-career crisis exposes the weakness in his
> character. His strengths are those of adolescence; he is playful, industrious,
> fair, enthusiastic, and open to new ideas. He has the adolescent's yearning
> for independence and ideals, but also the problem of facing his own
> limitations. More dependent on both others and the organization then he
> admits, the gamesman fears feeling trapped. He wants to maintain an illusion
> of limitless options, and that limits his capacity for personal intimacy and
> social commitment. (ibid., p. 107)

The typical gamesman is male, and his wife is always supportive; she is intelligent, competent, civic-minded, and success-oriented (ibid., pp. 116–18). Although not all of the founding presidents would fit the games- man mold or even identify with the analogy, the parallels are sufficient to warrant a comparison, thereby, one hopes, adding to the understanding of the role played by the early presidents.

Many of the early presidents fit the mold of the gamesman, for they too were competitive, innovative, independent (not bound by ties of traditional higher education), fast-moving, and flexible. (Many of these traits, which remain ingrained in today's presidents, are manifest in attitudes toward student enrollments. For example, often the first question presidents ask each other is "How is your enrollment?" Even in a time of decreasing numbers of high school students, too often a president's effectiveness is measured largely by enrollment growth or decline. Most presidents are very competitive about increasing enrollments: they show great innovation and flexibility when it comes to enrolling students, and brag when enrollments rise.)

The early presidents were, in every sense of the word, leaders on the make. Breaking the bonds of their blue-collar backgrounds (Vaughan 1986, pp. 7–15), these early leaders spent many hours dramatizing their ideas and motivating others to join the "crusade." Even the gamesman's need to control the situation was exemplified by a dogmatic, paternalistic approach to the presidency. And the founding president's wife (almost all of the founding presidents were male) was supportive, competent, and civic-minded to the point of sacrificing her own needs and career for the sake of her husband.

While Gardner's observations on the nation's early political leaders are helpful, and while the gamesman analogy is useful in understanding the founding community college presidents, times have changed. Now it is time to look at community college presidents in light of today's needs and expectations and in terms of the future.

THE SHIFTING FOCUS OF THE PRESIDENCY

New community college leaders tend to discount or disregard the considerable contributions of the founding presidents, even to the point of losing sight of the community college's recent history. (I recall mentioning, to the managing editor of a major publication devoted to the community college, Jesse Bogue's seminal 1950 book, *The Community College*. The editor's asked me, "Who is Jesse Bogue?") Today, a need exists to understand the community college presidency more fully and thus to appreciate the potential and limitations of the community college. In talking with new presidents, deans, and vice presidents, one hears the terms "leadership in transition" and "evolving leadership" used to describe the "new breed" of community college leaders. Too often these phrases are hollow indeed, for in contrast to the early leaders who focused on their roles as builders, today's leaders have no such focus. This lack of focus leaves a gap between the presidents of the past and the presidents of today, a gap that will extend into the future unless more focus is brought to the community college presidency. As a consequence, the role of the president in shaping the future of the community college is murky at best.

In some respects, the early presidents found it easier to accept, understand, and communicate their role than current presidents do, if for no
other reason than that their role as builder and salesman was largely defined for them. A founding president moved into an area, constructed
buildings, employed faculty, developed curricula, recruited students,
placed the teaching and learning process in motion, and spread the mission of the community college to anyone who would listen. Presidents,
faculty, staff, students, and society had a generally clear vision of what
a community college president did when buildings were going up daily,
enrollments and faculty were doubling annually, and state legislators supported community colleges even to the point of building their election
campaigns on this support. But a new concept of the presidency has not
evolved over the years, in spite of the talk about evolving leadership, an
understanding of the presidency has not transcended the gap between the
founding years—the building years—and today's presidency. Indeed, the
founding presidents were better at articulating the mission than today's
presidents, if for no other reason than that this was uppermost on their
list of priorities.

The words of a twenty-four-year veteran of the presidency, who was
the founding president of two community colleges and was also the chancellor of a major community college system founded by one of the legend-
ary figures of the boom years, convey a sense of the early years and what
may have gone wrong during the transition years.

> Some of the founding presidents, many of whom are leaving or have left the
> scene—I'm lucky, I was younger than most when I started—were
> charismatic, inspirational leaders who may not have known much about
> management. In the 1960s, we had to get out get the money, get the
> buildings built, and accommodate the hordes of students. We weren't
> worried about enrollments; we were worried about how to accommodate
> them. Very different then. I think some of my colleagues did not recognize
> the changes that had occurred and kept going the same way they had gone in
> the early years.

Although today's community college presidents still subscribe to the
vision of the community college developed during the 1960s and 1970s,
the president's role in achieving this vision is less clear than the role of the
founding presidents. Presidents during the earlier decades were literally
pioneers blazing the trails others were to follow; many of their decisions
were neither right nor wrong, for they were ground-breaking decisions
made in an environment that provided no basis for comparison, no perspective through which to judge their correctness. In contrast, the role of
today's president is blurred, for most presidents spend precious little time
today in communicating the mission (the vision), a role successful presidents must play if their community colleges are to achieve their full potential. Today's presidents spend too little time on introspection; they spend

too little time reflecting on the future of the community college as it relates to the larger society. As a result of the failure to replace the focus of the earlier years, a clear understanding of today's presidency eludes us.

BRINGING FOCUS TO THE PRESIDENCY

Based upon a large number of interviews with presidents and trustees, extensive reading related to the college and university presidency, and my own observations, I have concluded that three major functions should provide the focus for today's community college president: (1) managing the institution, (2) creating the campus climate, and (3) interpreting and communicating the institution's mission. I believe these functions can be carried out effectively only if the president views the institution broadly, including understanding the relationship among the three functions. Understanding the functions and their relationship to each other requires that the president be the institution's educational leader, for educational leadership is critical to establishing the campus climate, to understanding and communicating the mission, and to seeing that those who manage the day-to-day affairs of the institution keep its climate and mission central to all they do. Obviously, the three functions are never clear-cut, for they quite naturally overlap. For example, how the institution is managed has a profound effect on campus environment. The overlapping of the three functions dictates that the president's leadership be prominent in each of the three areas. This prominence demands that the president provide leadership to the entire college community and to important segments of the community at large and requires the president to be an educational leader.

The Functions Discussed

Today's community college president has outgrown the adolescence of Maccoby's gamesman. Just as the midcareer crisis exposed the weakness in the character of Maccoby's gamesman, the maturing of the community college has exposed some of the weaknesses of the current community college president. Like Maccoby's gamesman, many current presidents maintain the illusion of limitless options, best exemplified by the belief that the community college can be all things to all people, can solve all of society's ills. Like the gamesman, many of today's presidents have problems facing their limitations: they believe that they can and should be involved in all aspects of campus operations, being everywhere and speaking about everything.

While any number of scholars have written about the changing community college mission (see Deegan, Tillery, and associates [1985] for a discussion of what the authors refer to as the "fifth generation" in community college development), few have attempted to relate the role of the president to achieving the mission. The tendency has been to discuss functions in terms of management versus leadership or to categorize functions in terms of leadership functions and management functions. For example, Joseph Kauffman, a highly respected authority on the presidency and one greatly admired by this writer, discusses presidential functions by separating the leadership function from what he refers to as the management and control functions. He assigns communicating the mission largely to the leadership function (Kauffman 1980, p. 14). I maintain that the dichotomy drawn between leadership and management is a false one and tends only to confuse rather than enlighten. At times the most charismatic leader functions as a manager; at times the most bureaucratic president must lead. The following three functions bring focus to the presidency, especially when one considers the president in the context of educational leader.

Managing the Institution. The president is responsible for seeing that the institution is managed effectively and efficiently. The often-heard debate about whether an effective leader can be an effective manager is fallacious. The institution must be managed well, and it is up to the president to see that good management is carried out, regardless of how much of this function is delegated.

Management consists of more than filling out forms, making up class schedules, and meeting the payroll, for, as George Keller insists, "Management is to organizations other than the state what statecraft is to the state" (Keller 1983, p. 41). Keller believes that effective management requires leaders who motivate others, make good use of information, express ideas, and plan for the future. His effective manager is spirited, committed, and entrepreneurial, a risk-taker who is devoted to large objectives as well as to effectiveness (ibid., p. 68), characteristics associated with the effective president.

Management also involves resource allocation, which ultimately determines the college's mission. As manager, the president must see that policies and procedures are fair and that they are applied fairly and consistently; as manager, the president must see that everything flows from the institutional mission, including food services, buildings and grounds, instruction, student services, and so forth.

At times it seems to many, especially the faculty, that the president devotes too much time to management and too little time to his other major functions. Presidents devote considerable time to management primarily for two reasons: (1) poor management often gets the president into trouble, for everyone, especially the governing board, wants a well-managed institution; and (2) the management function produces visible results, thus giving the president a sense of accomplishment. The management function is the one that is most often discussed in the literature on higher education and is the one that many presidents tend to view as constituting the whole of leadership. While there is much more to the presidency than effective management, the successful president realizes that solid management is the foundation on which dreams must rest.

Creating the Campus Climate. The president has the primary responsibility for creating a campus climate in which students, faculty, and staff can achieve their full potential as learners, professionals, workers, and members of the college community. The president sets the tone and pace—establishes the campus mood—that other members of the college community can sense, identify with, and emulate. The climate should result in what one source refers to as a "spirit of place," a climate that can develop only through the "presence and proper working together of all the parts that make up the community of scholars, a *gestalt,* that is much more and much more powerful than the segmented parts" (Pullias and Wilbur 1984, p. 7). Making the case for the interrelationship between management and climate, the authors note:

> Evidently such a community can and usually does become very complex and thus must be administered. The key point in this connection is that all of this administrative activity should contribute to the production and maintenance of the best possible conditions or environment for carrying on the process of the higher learning. A minimum requirement is that no administrative behavior should threaten or damage the quality of that environment. (ibid., p. 6)

The answers to a number of questions can help gauge campus climate. Is the campus tone one of friendliness, of professionalism, of excellence in all things, of caring, of doing all that is possible to see that students learn, that teachers teach, and that staff members serve? Does the tone encourage experimentation? That is, do members of the college community not only have the right to try new things but also the responsibility, even if they occasionally fail? Does the pace accommodate change in an orderly and accepted fashion? Are there means by which all can participate in the governance of the institution? Does the climate encourage individual renewal and provides resources and avenues whereby faculty and staff can participate in the renewal process? Are financial and physical resources adequate not only to achieve the basic mission of the institution but also to achieve an edge of excellence in the teaching and learning process?

In setting the institutional climate, the president has the primary responsibility for ensuring a reasonable degree of balance between institutional, community, and individual concerns and needs. A reasonable balance can be maintained only if institutional expectations are discussed, defined, and communicated to both external and internal constituents, an often difficult task requiring the skills and knowledge of an educational leader. While maintaining a degree of balance, the president must constantly stimulate individuals and groups to greater achievements in thought and action, which will move the institution to new heights in its service to the community and to the individual. The president has the primary responsibility for maintaining institutional integrity in the curriculum, in institutional management, in external relationships, and in all college activities. And lest one forget, the president has the responsibility for the final decision, the ultimate responsibility.

Interpreting and Communicating the Mission. The third major function of the president is to communicate the mission of the college effectively and consistently to the college's various constituents: trustee, legislators, and members of the executive branch; leaders in business and industry, government, and the local community at large; other educators, students, faculty, and staff; and the general public. Through this function the president instills a sense of vision of what the institution is capable of becoming; in conjunction with the governing board, the president defines the purpose of the institution.

One of the most significant findings in my previous study of the community college presidency was that presidents, trustees, and others perceived a major failure of the community college to be the unwillingness or inability of its leaders, especially presidents, to interpret and articulate the institution's mission effectively, consistently, and positively to the college's various publics (Vaughan 1986, pp. 108–114). In articulating the mission, the president must realize that the college's constituents are marchers in a passing parade, rather than a stable, captive audience. Legislators, trustees, faculties, high school teachers, community college students, and presidents all change. Just as importantly, the community college mission changes in emphasis, if not in scope. So much of the college's present and future depends upon how well the mission is understood: funding, prestige in the community, employment of graduates, acceptance of transfer students by four-year institutions, coordination with high schools, acceptance of the mission by faculty, staff, trustees and, ultimately, the utilization of the college's services. Indeed, the president's own tenure in office may depend upon how well the college's mission is understood and supported, especially by trustees and legislators. Although community college leaders will never rid the language of the phrase "they don't understand us," presidents must work constantly to shrink the numbers falling under the rubric of "they."

A METAPHOR FOR THE PRESIDENCY[3]

One problem in bringing a focus to the community college presidency is the fact that most occupants of the office are unable or unwilling to view

[3]A portion of the following discussion was published in George B. Vaughan, "Balancing the Presidential Seesaw," Southern Association of Community and Junior Colleges, Occasional Paper no. 2, vol. 4, July 1986. Used with permission.

the position from any perspective other than from the trenches in which the daily battles of the college are fought. Presidents can understand how to manage the institution more effectively, create a more positive environment, and communicate the institutional mission more effectively if they can somehow place themselves at a vantage point from which to view and influence the overall activities and directions of the college. The use of a metaphor for the presidency may provide that vantage point and thereby offer a fresh way of looking at the position.

The metaphors and images used to describe the college and university presidency are seemingly limitless. Manager, missionary (especially appropriate in the case of the early community college presidents), politician, caretaker, facilitator, captain of the ship, man or woman on a tightrope, mediator, mayor, keeper of the zoo, clergyman, conductor of a symphony (made up of soloists, one cynic observed), person atop a platform, military commander, superentrepreneur, foreman, bookkeeper, and business executive (a favorite of many community college presidents) are some of the terms used to capture the essence of the modern-day college and university presidency. I have found that all of these words and phrases, and the images they connote, although useful in understanding the presidency, fail to describe the role adequately.

President Atop Seesaw

The image I feel most clearly captures the community college presidency is that of the president standing on top of a seesaw, directly above the fulcrum, with feet apart, legs slightly bent for balance and weight shifting gently from leg to leg, from one side of the seesaw to the other. On one side of the seesaw are students, faculty, administrators, support staff, and other internal constituents; on the other side are politicians, members of coordinating agencies, business leaders, board members, alumni, special interest groups, and other external constituents.

The primary role of the president is to keep the seesaw in proper balance, thereby ensuring good management, a positive climate, and a mission that is understood and supported by members of the college community and the community at large. Proper balance does not mean a lack of movement; to the contrary, it means keeping the seesaw constantly but gently moving at all times without permitting either end to become overloaded, for the college is not functioning properly when either end of the seesaw hits the ground too often or stays on the ground too long, or when movement ceases for a long period of time.

The effective president applies the proper amount of pressure (a positive act) by shifting weight to alternate sides of the seesaw as needed. When the presidential seesaw is out of balance, *as all are at times,* some constituents are left high in the air while others have their feet glued to the ground. Indeed, if the seesaw is out of balance for a prolonged period of time, the president ultimately loses his or her balance and slides down the seesaw. (The imagery of the president sliding from leadership is more accurate than falling, for the descent is usually gradual rather than sudden.) Once the slide begins, the president is no longer able to control his or her own destiny, much less the destiny of the college. Through applying pressure, the president rights the balance as quickly, efficiently, and painlessly as possible and keeps the seesaw in motion when external or internal forces attempt to bring it to a halt.

A Delicate Balance

The presidential seesaw, like the seesaw of one's childhood, is delicately balanced. Just as it does not take a three-hundred-pound person to throw the childhood seesaw out of balance, neither does it take a major crisis to throw the presidential seesaw out of balance. Applying pressure to maintain the proper balance is indeed a delicate undertaking, often requiring the sensitivity of an artist, the vigilance of a commanding officer, and the skills of a labor mediator. The pressure used to keep the seesaw moving might best be described as "dynamic tension," a phrase made famous by Charles Atlas, the boyhood idol of many early community college presidents. (Those who are not familiar with advertisements promoting Atlas' exercise program might prefer the term "creative tension" to describe the pressure required to keep the seesaw in motion.)

Although minor events, as well as major ones, can destroy the balance of the presidential seesaw, the greatest threat to presidential effectiveness is so insidious that it is overlooked by the board and often by the president: a potentially devastating situation results not from a major budget cut, not from a march on the president's office, and not from a major confrontation with the governing board. *The greatest danger to the college and the most telling signal that the president is not providing effective leadership is when the seesaw stops, when there is not enough activity (or tension) to keep it moving.*

Ironically, various individuals and groups temporarily prefer the calmness that comes from a lack of motion. The governing board often perceives the lack of motion as stability resulting from presidential leadership; politicians are often relieved to find that requests for funding for costly new buildings and programs have stopped; faculty members tend to perceive a lack of motion as satisfaction with the teaching and learning processes; and the president often views a lack of motion as an endorsement of presidential performance.

Presidents and trustees who are insensitive to a lack of motion or who promote or accept a prolonged state of inactivity are doing the college a disservice, for tensions are necessary if the college is to progress. Effective presidents work, not to stop the seesaw, but to see that most tensions are creative and that these tensions permeate every aspect of the college's operation, thereby keeping the seesaw in motion and the president in a position to influence the motion. Those presidents without the creative drive to keep the seesaw moving have outlived their usefulness; trustees who accept and endorse a lack of motion are not monitoring presidential and college performance as they should.

When the seesaw is out of balance, the president must serve as a countervailing force to those constituents or groups that are causing the imbalance. A word of caution is in order, however. Causing imbalance must not be viewed as analogous to causing trouble, for the imbalance may be caused by positive activities as well as by negative ones. For example, an outstanding program head may be performing in an extraordinary fashion but dominating campus activities to such an extent that the college's mission—the seesaw—is out of balance, a situation that cannot be tolerated indefinitely no matter how just the cause. (University presidents with major athletic programs are constantly faced with an imbalance caused by winning or losing teams.)

Although the president should not become involved with numerous day-to-day issues and activities, his or her leadership is nevertheless necessary to keep the total college in balance and accomplish its mission. Indeed, if the president is unable to see that the college is managed well, that the environment is positive, and that the mission is understood, the seesaw will be out of balance constantly and permanently. Stated another way, if enough problems, no matter how minor they appear to be, are allowed to stack up on each end of the seesaw, the seesaw will bow in the middle and ultimately snap, and with the snap goes the president's tenure in office and reputation as a leader, at least on the local campus.

Shifting Coalitions

Imbalance between the two sides of the seesaw is complicated by the tendency of groups and individuals on either side to join together in order to increase their influence or to "cross over" to the other side of the seesaw. J. Victor Baldridge, in his study of governance at New York University, developed a political model of university governance based on shifting coalitions resulting in new and constantly changing power blocks (1971). All community colleges have elements of Baldridge's political model, for internal constituents are quite adept at shifting their loyalty to groups that will enhance their cause. Because of shifting loyalties, a president must deal constantly with shifting coalitions. If a coalition becomes too strong, internal groups that are not members of the coalition are excluded from important governance decisions, an unacceptable situation if continued for a long period of time. When a coalition becomes too strong, the president must effect a compromise whereby its requirements are met or it is rendered less powerful if the college is to maintain its balance.

The perpetual shifting of the various constituent groups complicates the presidential balancing act even further. For example, a faculty woman's group may cross over and join an external group committed to establishing a child care center. On another day, the same woman's group may remain on its side of the seesaw and join with male faculty members to campaign for lower teaching loads. In some instances, the governing board may cross over and be drawn into internal conflicts. Crossover coalitions are especially difficult to deal with, for the president discovers that the normal alliances one might expect to find among internal groups, which he or she has become accustomed to dealing with, have now become even more complicated and that the movement of the seesaw has become highly irregular. As debates become heated, and especially if the governing board enters the discussion, the president is tempted to be drawn into the vortex of the debate, a position that is unacceptable if presidential leadership is to be effective. The president must keep some distance from the debate if he or she is to apply the proper amount of presidential pressure to keep the college from losing its balance.

Balancing the Mission: A Necessity

As has been suggested, one of the three major functions of the president's office is communicating the college's mission. In order to do this effectively, the president must see that the mission is balanced. For example, the ongoing debate over quality versus access must be viewed in light of the college's total mission and a balance between the two maintained. Open access serves little purpose if the students believe they are receiving a valuable education when in fact their degrees have little value because of the poor quality of the educational program. On the other hand, quality must not be used as an excuse to exclude numbers of individuals from those segments of society the community college was created to serve. The balancing act between quality and access is extremely difficult, yet critical, if the community college is to serve its diverse student body.

Metaphor as Reminder

The seesaw metaphor reminds one that the president fills the accepted supporting role associated with his office; however, it also reminds one that vital powers are exercised through the president's office. The president posed above the fulcrum is in a powerful position to influence the activities and direction of the college. If things are going well, the president can exert just enough dynamic tension to keep things interesting and exciting; if things are going poorly with any segment of the college, the president can shift the weight of the office to create just the right amount of tension to correct the problem. From atop the seesaw, the president can lead, effect compromises, keep things running smoothly, ensure that the college is fulfilling its mission, and bring a focus to the presidency. Or, the president can slide from grace. It is up to the president to see that the college remains in proper balance, for without proper balance neither the president nor the college can reach its full potential.

As college presidents are keenly aware, riding the presidential seesaw can be challenging, exhilarating, and even breathtaking. However, all presidents are equally aware that the ride can be bumpy, boring, and professionally fatal. Fortunately, most presidents can, to a large degree, determine the quality and, up to a point, control the duration of the ride by successfully balancing the presidential seesaw.

SUMMARY

Before continuing, a brief reiteration of some of the key points discussed in this chapter might be useful in preparing for subsequent chapters.

- In order to understand today's community college presidency more fully, it is useful and perhaps necessary to understand the role played by the founding presidents, individuals who were in every sense leaders on the edge of a great movement.
- In examining the role of the founding presidents, it is important to recognize their role in shaping today's community college philosophy and today's presidency.
- To understand the presidency today, it is necessary to recognize that the community college presidency has changed, that the building period has ended.
- Today's leaders need to understand and acknowledge that the role of the president is ill-defined and often lacks a focus.
- A thesis of this chapter is that focus can be brought to the presidency if presidents are primarily concerned with managing the institution, creating the campus climate, and communicating the mission.
- This chapter used the metaphor of the president atop the seesaw as a means of viewing the presidency from a vantage point other that of daily activities.

This chapter places the community college presidency in historical perspective. The following chapters bring the presidency more clearly into focus in terms of today and offer observations on the position that should be helpful to anyone interested in the community college presidency.

2

THE PRESIDENT AS EDUCATIONAL LEADER

The community college president should be the person at the college who is the educational leader. He or she should not be just an administrator, just a manager. The key words are educational leader.
      —a community college president

In the '80s, presidents must again become educational leaders in their institutions. . . . Without the president at the head of the line, the faculty will not follow.
      —Richard M. Cyert

When a president is more eager to sit down and discuss plans for revising the curriculum with a visitor than to show off new buildings, we can be pretty sure that he has strong educational aspirations.
      —Harold W. Dodds

. . . or when a community college president is more eager to discuss the curriculum than enrollments.
      —George B. Vaughan

Leading an institution of higher education is a complex and demanding undertaking, no matter what the size, location, or type of institution. The sheer task of administering such an institution demands all the time and energy one can devote to the task. Today's college and university presidents are undeniably busy men and women; consequently, the temptation exists to neglect what should be the most important aspect of the presidency: educational leadership.

17

The thesis of this chapter is that the effective community college president must be the institution's educational leader. This strongly implies that leadership in an institution of higher education is different from leadership in any other segment of society because the institution is different; therefore, the president should embody the characteristics that make institutions of higher education distinctive. The distinguishing characteristic of the president as the leader of an academic institution ought to be a devotion to and appreciation of scholarship, including the encouragement of scholarly activities by himself or herself and by others.

Community college presidents, while charged with many of the administrative duties faced by their four-year colleagues, have a greater obligation to see that the college responds to local educational needs than their four-year counterparts. It would seem to follow, then, that community college presidents should devote a great deal of time, energy, and influence to educational leadership at the local level. The ability of the community college president to influence the educational process is enhanced by the flexibility of the community college and by a more centralized approach to curriculum development than often exists in those colleges and universities where most curriculum changes come about through the various disciplines, departments, and schools.

Educational leadership is far from automatic for community college presidents, for while many opportunities for educational leadership are available to the community college president, the position has its share of frustrations and problems that militate against the president devoting sufficient time and energy to educational leadership. The community college president's agenda may be filled with local issues rather than global ones such as Star Wars research or investments in South Africa; nevertheless, educational leadership often takes a backseat to the day-to-day tasks that eat away at the president's time and energy. For example, dealing with a local political or social problem may require the same amount of time and energy from the community college president as a problem of a larger political or social nature may require from a university president. After all, an individual can worry about and deal with only so many issues, regardless of the size or type of the institution or the scope of the issue. However, since problems and issues faced by community college presidents are more local in nature, these presidents are offered many opportunities to communicate with the institution's various constituents through writing, speaking, and the media, in ways that clearly place the president at the center of educational leadership. To be the institution's educational leader, the president must, however, offer solutions to problems and issues that are compatible with the college's mission and that gain understanding and support from members of the college community and the community at large.

SETTING THE STAGE

Probably the best discussion of the president's need to be the institution's educational leader is Harold W. Dodds' 1962 book, *The Academic President: Educator or Caretaker?* Dodds argues that the president's office will become almost extinct if it loses its traditional character of educational leadership. Calling for a better definition of the president's position, the author argues that the office of president is suspended between two worlds, the world of relative simplicity and the new world of complexity (pp. v–vi). While the world of the community college president or any other academic president has never been simple, most presidents agree that the position is more complex today than in the past if for no other reason than that society itself is more complex.

While Dodds' two-worlds analogy oversimplifies the complexities of the presidency today, many of his observations are as relevant today as they were in the early 1960s. He writes regarding educational leadership:

> Obviously, to succeed, a president must be fired by a deep concern for education. It is equally observable that not all of them are. It follows that since presidents are chosen by trustees, trustees must be persuaded that supporting activities are only a part of the president's assignment, that his first responsibility is for the institution's educational growth and scholarly vigor. (p. 8)

Although Dodds sees no escape from the management–public relations roles most presidents face, he nevertheless holds out hope for educational leadership. He concludes that as the president ". . . transfers his center of gravity from housekeeping [daily administrative tasks] to education, he will only be replacing one set of pressures with another more acceptable set" (p. 9). His conclusion affirms that the president must not only preserve his educational leadership role but must also enhance the role, that the president must participate actively in framing and carrying out the teaching and scholarly activities of the institution (p. 2).

Dodds was writing in what many consider to have been the halcyon days of higher education, days that, viewed from today's perspective, left time for educational leadership. What about today? What are the forces that compel one to view educational leadership in a new light and that shape the agenda for the president as the institution's educational leader?

I would argue that there are two major movements in higher education that have caught the national attention and therefore dictate that the successful community college president devote more time and energy to educational leadership: (1) the critical examination of the college curriculum (what is taught) and (2) the new demands for the measurement of student achievement (what is learned). These movements, documented in the plethora of national reports on higher education, have drawn the focus away from fiscal and physical issues and back to the teaching and learning process; these forces have focused political discussions on the college curriculum to a larger degree than at any time since the launching of *Sputnik*. As a result of these movements, presidents who have been quietly at work as educational leaders for a number of years are suddenly in the news. Conversely, those presidents who have ignored the educational process are now challenged to consider what it means for a student to receive a degree from the college they lead and what, in measurable terms, the college experience adds to a person's life.

Presidents, and especially community college presidents who still view the community college curriculum as offering something for everyone, might profit from giving serious thought to Clark Kerr's statement that "In the final analysis, the curriculum is nothing less than the statement a college makes about what, out of that totality of man's constantly growing knowledge and experience, is considered useful, appropriate, or relevant to the lives of educated men and women at a certain point of time" (Kerr 1977, p. ix). Kerr observes that educators have never been totally satisfied with the curriculum, a curriculum that ". . . has been subjected to incessant, often conflicting, pressures and tensions from within and without the college since the founding of Harvard in 1636" (Kerr 1977, p. ix). In many respects, no segment of higher education is subjected to more tugs and pulls on the curriculum than community colleges, which experience demands from community needs of practically every description. By responding to the diverse forces that combine to create a community, the community college is faced with the difficult task of deciding what is "useful, appropriate, or relevant to the lives of educated men and women at a certain point of time" and in a certain geographic location.

Although current curriculum and student assessment reforms call attention to the educational process and, therefore, shape presidential leadership, limiting the president's educational leadership to these aspects of the college's operation would define it too narrowly. The effective community college president must do more than understand and endorse curriculum changes and evaluate the student's experience, no matter how important and relevant these are. *The successful president, as educational leader, must not only interpret the reforms in curriculum and student assessment to trustees, other educators, politicians, members of the college community, and the public in general, but must also continue to interpret and communicate the totality of the community college's mission to all constituents.*

Clark Kerr noted in a personal interview: "First of all, you [the president] have to know what is going on, you have to understand it, you have to prepare it in a way that other people can accept it and benefit from it. It's only the president who can set these standards and show his concern." That is, the president as educational leader interprets and communicates the college's entire needs—indeed, its reason for existence—to its constituents, including the need for continuing and increased funding for faculty, staff, supplies, equipment, and buildings; the need for faculty and staff development; the need for expanded programs and services; the need for eliminating programs and positions; and the need for ensuring that the community college is an integral part of the educational fabric of the community, the state, and the nation. The responsibility for communicating the mission has been a requirement of the academic president for centuries. By forcing the community college president to seriously question the curriculum and explain its effect on students, the current reform movements highlight the need for educational leadership. These movements, while offering excellent reasons for the president to become involved in curriculum changes, also offer the excuse, for most faculty members are more willing to accept (and even to expect) the president's involvement when curriculum issues enter the national arena.

EDUCATIONAL LEADERSHIP AS A FOCUS FOR THE PRESIDENCY

In Chapter 1 it was suggested that three primary functions fall under the umbrella of the president's office: seeing that the institution is well managed, creating the campus climate, and interpreting and communicating the college's mission. The three functions are never clear-cut; therefore, if presidents are to be effective, they must exercise educational leadership in all three areas, often simultaneously. For example, the management of funds plays a key role in setting the institutional climate and determining the institutional mission. How the mission is interpreted and communicated often determines what funds are available. Campus climate affects the instructional program and therefore the mission. The cycle continues.

If the role of the president as educational leader seems so obvious, why are presidents not devoting more time, energy, and thought to this role, a role some presidents never assumed and others abandoned in practice if not in theory?

Erroneous Interpretations and Mitigating Circumstances

A major reason some presidents have failed to emphasize educational leadership is that they have equated it with academic leadership. Indeed, in my previous study of the presidency, I found a number of presidents who were frustrated because they felt they were not viewed as the college's academic leader (Vaughan 1986, pp. 62–66), a function that rightly belongs to the academic dean.

Educational leadership should not be equated with academic leadership; therefore, it is a mistake for presidents to abandon educational leadership because they cannot and should not be the institution's academic

leader. While it was suggested above that the emphasis on student assessment and curriculum changes has forced the president to think about educational leadership, it is dangerous for the president to become overly
involved in the details of student assessment or curriculum reform.
Rather than dealing with the details of academic programs, presidents
should devote their time and energy to seeing that the institution is managed in a way that contributes to assessment and curriculum reform; to
seeing that the institutional climate not only permits changes but encourages them; to shaping and reshaping the vision and therefore the mission;
and to interpreting to both internal and external constituents the changes
taking place in teaching, learning, and the mission. Only through educational leadership can the president influence the thoughts and actions of
internal and external constituents. Only through educational leadership
can the president ensure that those who manage the day-to-day affairs of
the institution keep its climate and mission central to all that they do.
*Only through educational leadership can the president demonstrate,
through words and deeds, that an educational institution's reason for existence is the discovery, examination, analysis, organization, and transfer of knowledge.* Through educational leadership the president, in conjunction with the governing board, instills a vision of what the institution
is capable of becoming; through educational leadership the president defines and interprets the purpose of the institution.

Richard Cyert, president of Carnegie-Mellon University, suggested at
the beginning of the 1980s that the solutions to the issues facing higher
education all require strong leadership from the president.

> In the '80s, presidents must again become educational leaders in their
> institutions. Even fund-raising activities may have to take a back seat to the
> necessity of having the president function as an intellectual leader. In their
> actions and in their utterances, the presidents must embody the search of
> excellence that they want and need in faculty members. No longer can the
> president be strictly an outside person. The demands of the inside are going
> to overwhelm the demands of the outside. The president will need to write
> more and speak more to the faculty in large and small groups. . . . Without
> the president at the head of the line, the faculty will not follow. (Cyert 1980,
> p. 65).

Or as one community college president believes, "The leader of the future is going to have to be the person who stands between a field of research and operations; the leader must become an active translator in the
process, because change is coming more rapidly than in the past." The
president, then, must be the institution's educational leader.

A second reason that some presidents gave the role of educational
leader less attention is that, as community colleges developed, mitigating
circumstances caused presidents, especially founding presidents, to define their leadership role in ways that did not always encompass the

broader concepts of educational leadership. For example, founding presidents found it easier to hide behind the flurry of activities that accompanied the opening of a college than to face up to the need to exercise educational leadership; founding presidents spent most of their time "doing," not "reflecting." As a result, most founding presidents, in this aspect of the presidency, have been poor role models for those who followed them.

PREREQUISITES TO EDUCATIONAL LEADERSHIP

In 1959, Harold W. Stoke, then president of Queens College, wrote *The American College President,* which has become something of a classic in the field. Stoke discussed a number of qualifications and characteristics of the successful president, placing one qualification above all others:

> The most important qualification a college president can bring to his job is a philosophy of education. By a philosophy of education I mean nothing more than that he shall have thought about why the institution he presides over exists at all, for whom it is trying to provide education, and what kind of education it is trying to provide. . . . A college president without a philosophy of education is a pilot without navigation charts." (Stoke 1959, p. 161)

The successful president must have a vision of what the institution is, should be, and can become.

A philosophy of education forces one to focus on the institution's mission. Without a philosophy of education that is compatible with institutional mission, it is virtually impossible to interpret, shape, and communicate that mission, a mandate for the successful president. Without assuming the responsibility for interpreting and communicating the institution's mission—a mission the successful president helps to shape—to the college community and to the community at large, the president cannot be the institution's educational leader.

What are the prerequisites for developing an educational philosophy, interpreting and communicating the mission, and functioning as the institution's educational leader? One's academic discipline is not necessarily a prerequisite, for successful academic presidents have come from practically all disciplines.[1] In order to be the institution's educational leader, the president must be a scholar of higher education, regardless of what discipline is brought to the presidency. A scholar of higher education is

[1] I believe community college presidents should have at least a master's degree in an academic discipline or in a field such as business. While this may be viewed as a personal bias, from a practical point of view it seems important for the educational leader of an institution to meet the minimum requirements for teaching in the college which he or she is leading. Of course, there are many other arguments (acceptance by the faculty, for example) why the president should be a product of an academic discipline or a rigorous professional school, at least through a master's degree.

not simply one who reads journals devoted to higher education—although it is important that the president read the professional literature in the field—but rather one who recognizes that higher education does not exist in a vacuum, that it is influenced and often directed by economic, social, and political forces and trends. The scholar of higher education studies these forces and trends and relates them to the field of higher education. The ideal scholar of higher education would follow the examples set by David Riesman and Clark Kerr, both shrewd observers of social, political, and economic trends as well as of human nature. To be an effective scholar, one's education must continue throughout one's professional life; to understand higher education, presidents must commit themselves to the study of it as they would to any other discipline. If presidents are to be effective scholars of higher education, they must be more than historians, chemical engineers, psychologists, or members of any other discipline, although ideal presidents will stay in touch with their discipline to the extent possible. The study of higher education helps presidents place the college they serve and all of higher education in a perspective that makes sense for students, faculty, administrators, trustees, staff, the public in general, and themselves.

Scholarship: Key to Educational Leadership[2]

As presidents and other institutional leaders continue to evaluate and define the role community colleges play in the nation's system of higher education, they must realize that the failure to include scholarship as an important element in the community college philosophy erodes the images, indeed erodes the status, of these institutions among other institutions of higher education. As institutions dedicated to teaching and service, community colleges can never achieve their full potential without a commitment to scholarship. Without presidential leadership, the commitment to scholarship by the faculty and other administrators will rarely occur, and when it does, the president who is not a scholar will be an outsider rather than the institution's educational leader.

To test the need for the president to be a scholar, a definition of scholarship is in order. I see scholarship as the systematic pursuit of a topic, as an objective, rational inquiry involving critical analysis. It involves precise observation, organization, and recording of information in the search for truth and order. It is the umbrella under which research falls, for research is but one form of scholarship. Scholarship results in a product that is shared with others and that is subject to the criticism of individuals qualified to judge the product, whether it be a book review, an annotated bibliography, a lecture, a review of existing research on a topic, or

[2]Portions of the following discussion on scholarship were included in George B. Vaughan, "Scholarship in Community College: The Path to Respect," *Educational Record* (Spring 1988).

a speech that synthesizes the thinking on a topic. Scholarship requires one to have a solid foundation in one's professional field and to keep current with developments in that field.

The need for presidents to commit themselves to scholarship goes much deeper than defining the term. Community college presidents need to reflect more on the community college's past, present, and future. An examination of the past will reveal that community colleges fought hard and long to become a part of higher education, although "community" rather than "college" was the key concept emphasized by most community college leaders during the 1960s and 1970s. Today's community college presidents have given little thought to what it means to be an institution of higher education in the more traditional sense of the term. I believe the future will not only require that community college leaders devote more time and effort to interpreting and communicating what it means to be a college as defined by much of the rest of higher education and society, but will also see increased emphasis upon defining what the *college* experience means to the individual and to society.

Critical to understanding the relationship between scholarship and the community college philosophy is the recognition that the community college is first and foremost an institution of higher education. The lifeblood of any institution of higher learning must be a commitment to scholarship, for a commitment to teaching alone is not enough. Scholarship is the avenue through which the community college faculty member and administrator stay in touch with the academic enterprise; scholarship pulls us back to learning, back to the college's mission, back to the core of the enterprise. Scholarship, perhaps more than any other characteristic, distinguishes teaching and administering in an institution of higher education as a unique profession in our society, a profession that does not settle for a snapshot of current or past knowledge but rather views knowledge as dynamic and effective teaching and learning as requiring constant inquiry, learning, and interaction with emerging and existing knowledge. While many professionals outside the academic community engage in what is often referred to as lifelong learning, few pursue knowledge with an emphasis not just upon learning but upon teaching, critical analysis, and the interpretation of knowledge. Scholarship gives the community college professional legitimacy in the world of higher education.

However, community college presidents argue that they are products of pragmatism, not the ivory tower. Indeed, community college presidents can be justly proud of their pragmatic approach to the presidency, for in the past this approach has served them and society well. Although agreeing with Stoke that an educational philosophy is a prerequisite for the successful presidency, presidents need more than philosophy on which to build their house of the intellect. They need to be pragmatic as well as reflective; their philosophical stance must be grounded in pragmatism.

There are many practical, as well as philosophical, reasons for engaging in scholarship. As Ernest Boyer observes, "Scholarship is not an esoteric appendage; it is at the heart of what the profession is all about. All faculty, throughout their careers, should, themselves, remain students. As scholars, they must continue to learn and be seriously and continuously engaged in the expanding intellectual world" (Boyer 1987, p. 131). Presidents should understand that the discipline and thought required to be a scholar sharpen one's critical skills, skills that are required of the effective teacher and administrator. Only through critical review and analysis can presidents (and thus the colleges they lead) formulate positions on the issues of the day and in turn interpret those issues in a way that has meaning to members of the college community and ultimately to society. Critical review and analysis of the issues are required if community colleges are to receive adequate community support, funding, and students. Through scholarship presidents can ask and hope to find answers to the difficult questions the community college faces now and will face in the future.

Scholarship enhances a president's standing as a professional in a profession that reveres scholarship, if not always in practice, at least in theory. It produces competence in individuals and respectability among peers both inside and outside the community college field, a respect that is essential to membership in one's profession.

Community college presidents proclaim loudly and often that community college professionals do not engage in research. Rejecting research as a top priority for most community college professionals is, I believe, the correct stance. Too often, however, the debate over teaching versus research is used as a smoke screen for those administrators and faculty members who think that the lack of emphasis on research excuses them from pursuing scholarship. The president as educational leader is obligated to place the debate regarding research, teaching, and scholarship in its proper perspective. *The debate for the community college professional is not one of teaching versus research but rather one of the community college professional as teacher and scholar, as administrator and scholar, versus teacher or administrator only. Every community college professional must face this question: can the community college be an effective teaching institution without a commitment to scholarship by its administrators and faculty?* The president must play a key role in bringing about this commitment to scholarship, for without presidential leadership the commitment of the college as a whole will not occur.

Should the community college president be a scholar? The question is indeed rhetorical: the president who rejects the scholarly role rejects the very heart and soul of the academic enterprise. The president who is not devoted to scholarship cannot long endure as the institution's educational leader.

In a national survey of 75 community college presidents (63 responded) identified as leaders by their peers from across the nation, 10 presidents received 5 or more votes. Two of the 10 were well ahead of the remaining

8. Significantly for this discussion, the 2 receiving the most votes are presidents of colleges that are recognized nationally for their work in curriculum reform and assessment of student learning (Vaughan 1986, p. 201–2).

I interviewed one of the two presidents receiving the largest number of votes, and one of the questions I asked him concerned his views on educational leadership, especially in relationship to scholarship. This was his answer: "I think of my job as steering the institution within the framework of the world, the nation, and the community. Therefore, I believe it is my job to continue to learn, to do scholarly work, and to publish the results" (ibid., p. 190). Similarly, Warren Bryan Martin views the college president "as interpreter of the educational functions to various elements of the school's constituency. . . . [as] the balanced professional with the skills and spirit appropriate to institutional and societal leadership in our time" (Martin 1982, p.93). While not all presidents can or should publish the results of their scholarship, the effective president must nevertheless be a "balanced professional with the skills and spirit appropriate" to leadership now and in the future, who steers the "institution within the framework of the world, the nation, and the community."

The successful president of the future must be a scholar, for without a commitment to scholarship, educational leadership will falter. Without educational leadership from the president, the community college will be ill-defined and misunderstood by much of society. It will never achieve its rightful place among institutions of higher education or its full potential as an institution.

THE PRESIDENT AND EDUCATIONAL LEADERSHIP

Can the president assume the role of educational leader without becoming overly involved in the day-to-day activities of the college's academic program? Can the president serve as educational leader without appearing to usurp the prerogatives of faculty members and academic administrators? Obviously, I believe that the president can and should serve as the institution's educational leader and that, as suggested, educational leadership is more than just academic leadership.

A commitment to scholarship is one way presidents can visibly demonstrate that they understand the academic enterprise and their own role in leading an academic institution. The following suggestions are ways in which the president can play a leading role in bringing about a commitment to scholarship among members of the college community, thereby fulfilling this important aspect of educational leadership.

Leadership by Example

The concept of leadership by example is as old as the discussion of leadership itself. Yet, many presidents insist that they simply do not have time for scholarship. (Many faculty members make the same excuse.) Other presidents are excellent scholars but simply have not made this fact known to the college community. Neither situation offers an example worthy of emulation by other members of the college community.

Presidents should prepare their speeches dealing with the issues faced by the college, especially those they present to the faculty, according to accepted scholarly practices, for even the most enthusiastic faculty tires of the same redundant pep talks given by many presidents year after year. Copies of speeches should be made available to members of the college community. While it is not necessary to publish the results of one's scholarship (many scholars argue otherwise), it is nevertheless useful if the president occasionally publishes a scholarly piece, either in the local newspaper (the op-ed page is an excellent avenue for such publications), an internal document, or a professional publication. Presidents should suggest articles and books to members of the college community for their consideration. Through actions such as these, presidents are not only acknowledging that they are members of a profession and that the profession carries certain responsibilities that go beyond most positions in society, but they are also acknowledging that as the institution's leader they must embody the distinguishing characteristics of their profession, one of which is scholarship. Presidents who are practicing scholars lead by example and thereby help create a climate on campus that promotes scholarship.

Scholarship as a Part of the Rewards System

The most obvious way of enhancing scholarship is to make it an important part of the community college philosophy, a part of the rewards system, which can be achieved only with the president's endorsement and support. Scholarship should be an important consideration in granting tenure and academic rank. While there is some danger in this approach (community colleges must not fall into a "scholarship or perish" syndrome), the payoff in professionalism would be worth the risk. Including scholarship in the promotion and tenure process will make it impossible to separate scholarship from the role of faculty and administrators within the college and will make it impossible to separate scholarship from the community college philosophy.

Forums Devoted to Scholarship

Not all community colleges have funds for faculty to travel to professional meetings in order to keep abreast in their fields. Moreover, some faculty members do not attend professional meetings even when funds are available. One way for the president to promote scholarship is to institute a forum devoted to scholarship whereby faculty and administrators demonstrate their commitment to and their accomplishments in their field of scholarly activities. These forums could be especially important to the over five hundred small and often rural community colleges that suffer from the provincialism that results, in part, from their location and size. The forum, which can be an exhilarating form of renewal for faculty and administrators, should be conducted in the best academic tradition, with discussion, criticism, and questions after each presentation. The forum would make it possible for community colleges to be the leaders in a trans-disciplinary approach to scholarship, for rarely would the scholarly forum be conducted for members of just a single discipline, as is often the case on university campuses and almost always at professional meetings. Rather, all faculty members and administrators who are interested would be encouraged to attend and participate. The president should demonstrate a commitment to scholarship by making one of the earliest presentations to the forum, if not the first.

Leadership in Professional Renewal

Every president I have ever talked with about professional renewal believes that it is a right and a responsibility of the community college professional. Most presidents I have talked with admit that they have never taken a sabbatical. Indeed, most presidents do not take the vacation to which they are entitled, much less a sabbatical. For example, on the average, presidents take only 13 of the 21 days of vacation they earn each year; 44 percent take fewer than 10 days each year (Vaughan 1986, p. 213). Presidents can lead the way by taking some time away from campus to pursue scholarly activities. In addition, released time, summer employment other than teaching, study, and other avenues should be supported by the president and open to all faculty and administrators for the purpose of scholarly growth.

Pride in the Community College

Presidents must lead the way in dispelling the image that community colleges are second best in the higher education community, with practically all other members of the academy being first. Once scholarship becomes a part of the everyday scene on campus, community college professionals will find that they are not only as capable of doing scholarly work as their four-year counterparts, but that they—community college professionals—are bringing the same pragmatic approach to scholarship that they have brought to so much else; that they are doing scholarship as well as talking about it. This accomplishment alone will be unique enough in higher education to warrant the attention of all academics engaged in the pursuit of truth and knowledge. But until community college presidents take the lead in changing current expectations, attitudes, and practices toward scholarly activities, scholarship will remain low on the community college's agenda and the president cannot be fully effective as the institution's educational leader.

EDUCATIONAL LEADERSHIP IN PERSPECTIVE

During the 1960s and the early 1970s, the popular image of the university campus, while inaccurate as a generalization, was one of armed policemen and national guardsmen, occupied buildings, and general disarray on campuses culminating in the tragedy at Kent State University. The presidents were caught in the middle. Not only did faculty and students question presidential leadership, so did society as a whole. Works such as Cohen and March's *Leadership and Ambiguity* (1974) denied that colleges and universities needed strong presidents. Christopher Jencks and David Riesman's *The Academic Revolution* (1968) and the studies on academic governance by J. Victor Baldridge and others left little doubt that the faculty, while not in control of the academic enterprise, would never again be content to sit idly by and permit administrators and governing boards to dominate academic governance.

While some few presidents such as Theodore M. Hesburgh of Notre Dame University and William Friday of the University of North Carolina not only survived the difficulties of the era but seemed to thrive during the period of campus turmoil, neither effectively made the case for strong presidential leadership, beyond serving as an example. Although Friday was quoted often and the few writings of Hesburgh were sought out as rare jewels to be coveted as much for their scarcity as for their wisdom, positive writings on the college and university presidency were quite scarce. Even Clark Kerr's classic, *The Uses of the University,* was often misunderstood in reference to the presidency largely because of his use of the word "mediator" in describing the primary role of the president.

While it would be an overstatement to suggest that a synthesis has been reached by any segment of higher education or by the public that the academic president must be a strong leader, recent writings indicate that the pendulum has swung away from the focus on "leaders" who do not lead. For example, in 1982 Louis T. Benezet asked the question "Do Presidents Make A Difference?" His conclusion was that they could and should (Benezet 1982, pp. 11–13). In 1984 a study directed by Clark Kerr for the Association of Governing Boards of Universities and Colleges answered Benezet's question in the affirmative in a volume entitled *Presidents Make a Difference.* Kerr and Marian Gade further emphasized the positive side of the presidency in their 1986 volume entitled *The Many Lives of Academic Presidents: Time, Place and Character.* Meanwhile, James Fisher's *The Power of the Presidency* built a compelling case for a return to the strong presidency.

Although the community college presidency is not the central subject of any national and regional reports on curriculum reform and student assessment in higher education, strong presidential leadership is central to carrying out many of the recommendations of these reports. Indeed, it is unlikely that campus reform will occur without the president assuming the role of educational leader.

Significantly, leaders such as Ernest Boyer and Derek Bok have spoken out on the need for reform in higher education. Bok admits that professors are the central figures in the modern university but believes that strong educational leadership is still needed if major reforms in higher education are to come about (Bok 1986, pp. 191–201). Previously little-known and never-before recognized institutions such as Northeast Missouri State University and Alverno College have reached stardom because of the work they have done and are doing in the assessment of student learning. Miami-Dade Community College captured national attention with its work in curriculum reform and student assessment.

The conclusion of this chapter is that the time is right for community college presidents to assume the role of educational leader. While the opportunistic and pragmatic decades of the 1960s and 1970s were exciting ones for community college leadership, it is now time for presidents to put those years behind and to concentrate their energies on current issues, issues emanating from deciding what should be taught and what should be learned.

In his Pulitzer Prize–winning volume *The Age of Reform*, Richard Hofstadter offers advice to those who long for the golden age of populism; his advice might be helpful to those who long for the golden age of community college development. Hofstadter writes:

> In truth we may well sympathize with the Populists and with those who have shared their need to believe that somewhere in the American past there was a golden age whose life was far better than our own. But actually to live in that world, actually to enjoy its cherished promise and its imagined innocence, is no longer within our power. (Hofstadter 1955, p. 328)

It is no longer within the power of current community college leaders to build new campuses almost weekly, to double or triple enrollments annually, to recruit new faculty and administrators at an unprecedented pace, and to ask for and receive funds to support such growth. It is within the power of current community college presidents to exercise the educational leadership required to see that the buildings are used to support the institutional mission, that students get the education they deserve, that faculty and administrators provide the teaching that is required, and that legislators are aware of what community colleges are achieving in the teaching and learning process. For the president to fail to fulfill the role of educational leader is to fail to keep the basic purpose of the institution before all constituents and therefore to fail to achieve the potential of the presidency.

3

THE MYSTIQUE OF THE PRESIDENCY

The outstanding characteristic of a leader is his uniqueness. A leader is a person who invents a leader.
—Daniel Boorstin

I pretended to be somebody I wanted to be and I finally became that person. Or he became me. Or we met at some point. It's a relationship.
—Cary Grant

I don't think the expenditures have been out of line. I have tried to do what a college president is supposed to do.
—Robert L. Green, Former President, University of the District of Columbia

The trouble with John Wayne was that he believed he was John Wayne.
—Kirk Douglas

After serving as a community college president for almost seventeen years and after studying the presidency for the past seven years, I have concluded that community college presidents spend too much time and energy dealing with day-to-day affairs and too little time standing back and examining the enterprise they are leading and their roles as leaders. Presidents tend to see their roles as action-oriented, pragmatic ones that leave little time for reflection, analysis, scholarship, and setting goals. The pragmatic nature of the office causes too many presidents to confuse activity with leadership, which leads to too much involvement and too little thinking. The successful president of the future must spend more time creating a vision for the institution and identifying trends and issues in the broader society that will affect that vision. In order to find the time and intellectual energy required to create the vision, the successful president of the future must place some distance—physical, intellectual, and, to a degree, psychological—between the office of the president and the college's various constituents. Stated another way, the successful community college president of the future must cultivate the mystique that has been historically accorded four-year college and university presidents and that has worked to their advantage.

THE NEED FOR A MYSTIQUE

Mystique, as used in this chapter, is meant to convey the message that community college presidents need to step back and evaluate their roles more carefully, especially their roles as leaders and symbols of the college, for too often these roles are not well defined and therefore not well understood. In recent years most community college presidents have come to realize that the community college cannot and should not try to be all things to all people. Presidents should likewise admit that they cannot be all things to all people, cannot be everywhere at once, cannot furnish all the answers or even all of the questions. By recognizing their limitations, presidents can extricate themselves from the mundane activities of the campus and community. They can then devote their time and energy to creating a presidency that places the position clearly in the forefront of campus leadership, yet removes it from the daily tinkering with too many things that are much better left to other members of the college faculty and staff.

Mystique as used here is not an abstract concept; rather, by distancing themselves from the daily routine, presidents can enhance their effectiveness by making it clear that when they speak, they are speaking as leaders of their institutions, as presidents.

Mystique as used here is to be distinguished from aloofness. It implies an attitude toward the office of the president and not toward any individual president; it implies a concept and habits of leadership. Mystique means it is important to back off when it is inappropriate for the president's office to be involved. Unlike aloofness, it in no way implies that the president is unapproachable or all-powerful. To the contrary, mystique is perfectly compatible with James MacGregor Burns' belief that the effective leader is inseparable from the goals and needs of the followers (Burns 1978, p. 19). Aloofness, on the other hand, implies a lack of interest and a lack of feeling for the enterprise. Aloofness has an air of detachment, an air of indifference, which flies in the face of the effective president as depicted in this volume.

One way of approaching the presidency is to maintain that the president act only when it is inappropriate or impossible for others within the institution to do so. Approaching the position in this manner removes the presidency from many routine activities, thereby making the president less available (and less vulnerable) to the college community and to the community in general. Once removed from routine activities, the president has more time and energy for thinking, for defining college-wide issues, and for serving the college community and the community at large more effectively in dealing with the issues that require presidential attention. Defining the position in this manner automatically builds the potential for mystique into the presidency.

BACKGROUND

A brief look at the past is helpful in understanding why the community college presidency has developed as it has. At one period during the 1960s, community colleges were opening at the rate of almost one a week. Over three hundred presidents were founding presidents, and they were new to the office. It was not unusual for a new president to move into town and find that the proposed community college had nothing to begin with but a name, and in some cases not even that. Presidents bought or borrowed typewriters and other basic equipment and supplies; they rented space for temporary offices and classrooms; they hired the first staff and faculty; and they supervised ground-breaking ceremonies and construction projects. The words ubiquitous and pragmatic best described these presidents. Indeed, rather than defining their position in terms of a lack of action, many of the early community college presidents prided themselves on being available at all times and on their willingness to make an immediate decision independent of the thinking of others.

Looking back, the objective observer can see that the position lost much of its mystique because the president was too involved in too many activities. Yet, we founding presidents had to produce results quickly and had to be highly pragmatic, for there probably was no other way of opening the colleges as effectively and efficiently in such a short period of time. If a price was paid, it was a small one in light of the successes of the early presidents and the achievements of the colleges they founded. But times and needs have changed from the days of building new colleges and so must the approach to the presidency, for unless the president understands and defines the position in light of today's needs, it is likely that position will never achieve it potential for leadership.

Partly because so many colleges opened in so short a time, no group of leaders in the history of higher education was more available to their constituents then were the early community college presidents. Ubiquity rather than focus was the order of the day. Taking their text from the

Bible, community college presidents proclaimed that where two or three are gathered together there they will be also. Or, as one president boasts: ''Wind me up, give me an audience, and I will talk on anything, anytime, anywhere.'' Founding presidents, who were rightly expected to spread the community college gospel to all people, set the tone and pace for the ubiquitous presidency; later presidents followed suit, often without question.

Besides the need to ''sell'' the community college in its early years, many presidents found that their blue-collar backgrounds presented psychological blocks that made it difficult to act ''presidential'' in a traditional sense, for positions of high leadership in academia or elsewhere were not part of their heritage (Vaughan 1986, pp. 10–13). Moreover, serving as presidents of the ''people's college,'' with the expectations inherent in such a name, make it difficult both psychologically and physically to step back from the presidency more than a few steps. As a result, many presidents have been on the firing line too often, too long, and too needlessly, thereby making it difficult for them to deal with the larger issues facing the community college and the community college presidency.

In contrast to community college presidents, most four-year college and university presidents step into years of tradition when they assume the presidency, thereby gaining the prestige, distance, and mystique that have accumulated over a number of years and a number of presidencies. Indeed, if the predecessor was highly successful and had a relatively long tenure in office, the new four-year president may find that, by simply assuming office, he or she has prestige far beyond anything which could be created during one tenure in office, in sharp contrast to the situation that exists when starting a college from the beginning. Compare the images of the four-year presidencies that have evolved over the years—and in some cases over centuries—with those of founding community college presidents who had little or no tradition on which to build. Even in those four-year institutions that have had only moderate success, the president benefits from a sort of halo effect resulting from the public's perception of a college president. In contrast, no silver mace, no presidential medallion, and relatively little mystique came with the office of the new community college president.

In addition to the lack of a presidential tradition, the greatest period of community college growth was during the 1960s, a time in which many academic traditions were challenged. Graduation ceremonies lost much of their symbolism; students used the occasion to challenge both tradition and authority. On some campuses, student radicals prohibited presidents from occupying their offices; on other campuses presidents were prohibited from leaving them. The average length of presidential tenure dropped, as did presidential prestige. While the community colleges typically were not the immediate target of protesters, they nevertheless felt the impact of the larger movements in higher education and in society. In addition, many community college presidents were determined to make the community college the most open of all institutions during the most open period in the nation's history. The people's college democratized not only higher education but the presidency as well. While much good was done during the heady days when community colleges opened at the rate of one a week, they were not good years for establishing the mystique of the presidency.

Another important symbol of the presidency, a formal inauguration, was denied many community college presidents during the 1960s and 1970s. Without an inauguration, the president was never bestowed with the responsibilities, privileges, and symbols of the office, was never given a public ceremony bestowing what James Fisher refers to as legitimate power. Fisher believes that the legitimate power of the leader makes the use of other forms of power more acceptable to followers (Fisher 1984, pp. 33–37). In the early years (and today in many instances), rather than receiving legitimate power during a dignified ceremony performed before colleagues and community, the community college president's legitimate power came from a set of rules and regulations, many of which he or she wrote. Faculty members who had been schooled in the traditions of the post–World War II university and who were at the front edge of the academic revolution which, according to Jencks and Riesman (1968), led to faculty hegemony, did not appreciate, approve of, or understand this approach, although most governing boards not only approved the seemingly efficient system but applauded the immediate results it produced.

Should community college leaders of the 1960s and 1970s have been more concerned with the traditions and ceremonies associated with colleges and universities? More specifically, should presidents and board members have been more concerned with the symbols historically associated with the office of the academic president, assuming that symbols enhance the president's ability to serve the college more effectively? Probably. As one veteran president remarked,

> I thought presidential inaugurations were silly twenty years ago. Now I think we missed the boat by not adopting more of the symbolic practices that go with the office of president at most four-year institutions. I think that an inauguration tells the public and the faculty that the president is the institutional leader. I do not think the symbolism is lost and therefore is needed. Today, if I were to change positions, I would want an inauguration and believe it would help establish my presidency and bring prestige to the office.

In the 1960s and early 1970s it was difficult, if not impossible, for community college presidents to create a presidential image that had any degree of mystique. But society's attitude toward leadership has changed, and it is now time to bring a sharper focus to the community college president's role as institutional leader; it is now time to cultivate a mystique about the presidency; it is now time to shed some of the images and practices handed down from the founding presidents. By choosing more carefully the issues to which they devote their time, their energy, and the prestige of the office, presidents can increase the efficiency of the position and thereby enhance the image and effectiveness of the community college in American society.

DISTANCE AND THE PRESIDENCY

Clark Kerr and Marian Gade, in discussing presidents of urban community colleges, note that, "These presidents are on the social firing line where rich meet poor, where race meets race, where unions meet the public, where special interest group meets special interest group" (Kerr and Gade 1986, p. 167). While Kerr and Gade paint a less-than-desirable picture for many urban presidents, the image of the urban president constantly bumping into the community is typical of all community college presidents, no matter what the location or how desirable the position. In rural areas, for example, presidents are expected to assume a number of social and civic responsibilities that are not required or expected of presidents in urban areas or at four-year institutions.

Although many of the president's contacts are more subtle than dealing with unions, special interest groups, and other high-profile encounters, they nevertheless take their toll in time, energy, and sheer "maintenance costs." For example, most community college presidents belong to a service club, serve on a number of community forums, take calls from the media, and serve on the chamber of commerce board, or at least on a committee of the board. The list of community activities is literally endless. Many of the activities are not only desirable but necessary to a successful presidency. Viewed separately, each of these activities and memberships appears to enhance the presidency. Moreover, all of them are honorable and are symbolic of good citizenship.

On the other hand, once the various memberships and activities are seen in their entirety, they often become overwhelming. When the burden on the president becomes too great, a sort of reverse synergism occurs: the whole not only does not exceed the sum of the parts but the whole of the presidency becomes less than the parts. Endless community activities place the president in the position of participating in too many routine activities that are of too little benefit to the college.

In addition to community and home activities, many community college presidents function on campus in a way that detracts from the mystique of the presidency. Even today, some presidents act almost alone in deciding what faculty to employ, what instructional equipment to pur-

chase, who should be promoted and, in some cases, who should be re-
tained and who should be dismissed. Even today some presidents participate in day-to-day negotiations with union representatives. Even today,
some presidents approve all faculty travel requests. All of this is happening in spite of the great strides many campuses have taken toward participatory governance and shared authority. However, by becoming overly
involved in the daily activities of the college, presidents destroy the mystique of the presidency even on their own campus and lessen their effectiveness.

A strong argument for presidents to place distance between themselves
and their constituents is made by James Fisher in his 1984 book, *The
Power of the Presidency*. Fisher recommends that presidents place themselves squarely and solidly on the presidential platform and stay there.
Occupancy of the presidential platform creates an aura of distance and
mystery about the presidency, a distance that results in the president being able to exercise power more effectively (pp. 1–13). A key to assuming
the presidential platform and using the position to enhance presidential
effectiveness is what Fisher refers to as charismatic power. In calling for
presidents to develop charisma, Fisher concludes that the three principal
conditions for charisma are distance, style, and perceived self-confidence. The most important, and most clearly documentable of the three
is distance for, according to Fisher, day-to-day intimacy destroys illu-
sions (pp. 39–43), destroys what I refer to as mystique.

Fisher states that it is unwise for the college president to have intimate
relationships with members of the faculty (p. 45). (David Riesman in a
personal interview wryly observed that "Many presidents have no problem with that particular advice because faculty keep their distance from
them.") For a number of reasons, most community college presidents
have no major problems with becoming too intimate with the faculty. Few
community college presidents are "first among equals" in the sense that
the term is used to describe the renowned scholar who has left the depart-
ment (but never the discipline, at least in theory) to become president,
for most community college presidents have degrees in education rather
than the traditional disciplines (Vaughan 1986, p. 19). In addition, administrative structures, which are often more bureaucratic, formal, and rigid
than they are perceived to be at four-year institutions, tend to place psychological distance between the president and faculty at community colleges. But achieving distance in the way Fisher uses the concept is not as
simple as working in a bureaucracy would make it seem.

The somewhat formal bureaucratic structure that keeps the president
at a distance from the faculty at the same time often encourages the president to become overly involved in the details of the college's operation,
thereby destroying any advantages that could conceivably accrue from
the distance provided by the college's organization. The dilemma created
by the college's organization was clearly seen with the movement toward

more participatory governance that occurred on many community college campuses in recent years. Participatory governance illustrated that psychological distance existed between the president's office and the faculty, for many presidents were uncomfortable with the idea of faculty as colleagues.

Is Fisher's concept of the presidential platform relevant to the community college presidency? Yes, for certainly this chapter owes much to Fisher's well-conceived and well-stated belief that college presidents need to place more distance between themselves and their various constituents than in the past. But at times Fisher pushes his argument beyond the pale of the current status of many community college presidents. For example, he cautions presidents to "never, never get off that presidential platform" (1984, p. 12). Most community college presidents, however, have never planted themselves squarely on the presidential platform, never thought about the need to concern themselves with a presidential mystique. For community college presidents to change their habits suddenly would appear to be erratic and perhaps irrational. The movement from the trenches to the presidential platform cannot take place in one giant leap; a more effective approach would be gradual disengagement from selected current practices. People want steadiness in a leader, not erratic behavior. For community college presidents who have spent most of their careers working with day-to-day problems to appear to succumb to the ivory tower of isolation would fly in the face of their past behavior and would create confusion rather than healthy distance; moreover, even the appearance of isolation is unacceptable in a college devoted to community both in the narrow and larger sense of the term.

In the personal interview cited above, David Riesman offered his views on applying the Fisher thesis. He observed that, "For one thing, presidents have to do what is comfortable for them, and for a shy, withdrawn, extremely intelligent person who will establish his or her legitimacy only over a period of time to pretend to behave like Jim Fisher would be crazy, or to behave like John F. Kennedy or whatever." I would add that presidents must also do what is comfortable for the college. For a president to assume the presidential platform in Fisher's sense, in a college that is crying for personal contact and even intimacy, would be suicide for the president as well as the college. In the final analysis, presidents should use good judgment in deciding how much distance to place between themselves and their constituents.

Fisher's thesis, as with the thesis of this chapter, must be approached with common sense, an approach with which Fisher would readily agree, I believe. Therefore, any president concerned with placing more distance, especially psychological distance, between the presidency and constituents should keep the concept in perspective, for as John W. Gardner observes, the research on how much distance the leader should place between himself or herself and those being led is inconclusive (June 1986,

p. 10). Each president, then, needs to ask how much familiarity it takes to breed contempt, or at least to lessen presidential effectiveness, and act upon the answer.

One Step Back: Delegation

The oldest and most basic approach to developing a presidential stance and potentially adding to the mystique of the presidency without isolating the office is to delegate responsibility and authority to others within the organization. While this chapter is not a treatise on effective management, some observations on delegation serve to remind the president that delegation comes hard, especially early in one's presidency. According to one study of the presidency,

> Some presidents have difficulty delegating authority; hence their days are swamped with attention to details that would best be left to others. Further, in spite of the enormous pressures on them, they often seem to be unable to budget their time. For instance, some presidents see many people who could be seen by other representatives of the institution; also the amount of time spent in these visits does not always seem to be warranted. (Benezet, Katz, and Magnusson 1981, p. 14)

The authors go on to suggest that the flaw noted in regard to delegation is a remediable flaw. "Sophistication in administration, like sophistication in teaching, is for almost every president an acquired art, an art that can be further cultivated" (ibid., p. 14).

One president's thinking is in concert with the above observations regarding delegation. He confesses:

> I think I have a better handle on delegation now than I did a few years ago because I have gone through the hoops in terms of community and professional involvement. But I'm still run ragged at times trying to please the multiple constituencies of the presidency. I think I have now realized that that's impossible. I'm trying to narrow my focus in a number of ways. One, I try to involve myself only with things that are of interest to me and that can make a difference in the college; two, I delegate, get other people involved. Now the president has to be the president, but staff members can and should do a good bit of the preliminary work on a project thereby saving me from going in a million directions at once. In the same regard, in the early years all questions from the media were referred to me for my comment. I now delegate many of the questions to others. This makes them feel good, makes them more responsible, and responsive, and gives them a bit of ego satisfaction. Meanwhile, it leaves me time to do other things.

The president must be sure that when tasks are delegated, it is the president's office and not the college that is removed from community activities. It is dangerous for the president to keep too great a psychological distance from the faculty, administrators, trustees, and staff. Indeed, there is some danger inherent in saying no to requests from community members, especially if the reasons for saying no are not clear and if saying no removes the college from some aspect of the community with which it should be associated. One highly successful president from a metropolitan area speaks to this point.

> In regard to community involvement, I think you have to pick and choose. I'm probably asked to serve with a hundred different groups. The first thing I do is ask myself if having the college represented on a particular board will really help the college. If so, I thank people for the call but suggest that they really don't want the president of ——— Community College; rather, I suggest that what they want is the presence of ——— Community College. I will then provide them with the most outstanding individual at the college who has knowledge in the area they seek. That person will serve on the board. I then offer to work with that individual and, if appropriate, will attend the annual meeting of the organization.

When the president assigns a task to a member of the college community, the college as well as the office of the president is represented while at the same time the president is free to pursue other activities more appropriate to his office. The mystique of the presidency is enhanced, thus permitting the president to function more fully as the institution's leader.

The effective president magnifies his or her influence and sense of presence by delegating responsibility and authority to others, including members of the community. However, one should realize that delegation alone will not necessarily add to the mystique of the presidency. Indeed, the concept as presented here is much more complex than the simple act of delegating, for delegating alone comes across somewhat as the textbook answer to a complex issue. For example, after presenting the concept of the mystique of the presidency to a group of my presidential colleagues and other community college educators, I was approached by a young man—very young in terms of experience—from the state-level office of a community college system. He told me: "Everyone knows that the good manager keeps his distance from those he manages." While I felt that somehow the young man missed the point (the phrase "those he manages" had tipped his hand), he nevertheless made me realize that some people could reduce a very complex concept to the relatively simple task of delegating tasks or "managing people." Nevertheless, effective delegation does offer the president more time for dealing with those things that require presidential attention. But how can one develop a presidential stance that goes well beyond the act of delegating? How can one develop a style that keeps presidential involvement on a level that increases presidential effectiveness while at the same time not giving the appearance of aloofness?

Adding Mystique

It was suggested earlier that the mystique associated with the presidency results, in part, from the manner in which the position is approached. The following suggestions, if followed, should enhance the mystique of the presidency and in turn enhance presidential effectiveness.

Shed Old Habits. The cliché "old habits die hard" is never truer than when speaking of a dean who assumes the presidency. The academic dean may well enjoy working on curriculum and instruction more than anything in the world. If this is the case, he or she should remain an academic dean, for the effective president cannot spend a great deal of time working directly with curriculum and instruction. The same is true to even a greater degree of the financial and student services deans. Once someone from these positions assumes the presidency, he or she must shed the preoccupation with the relatively narrow focus of the former position or else will find it impossible to develop the mystique of the presidency.

Accept Only Presidential Assignments. Before accepting a committee or task force assignment, either in the academic community or in the community at large, the president should find out who else will be on the committee. If membership consists of academic vice presidents or deans from four-year institutions, the president should not agree to serve unless there is a compelling reason for doing so. Rather, the task should be assigned to the academic dean. The same reasoning applies to community commitments. If a community forum is made up of midlevel managers such as personnel directors, training directors, office managers, high school principals, and similar individuals, the president should not accept membership but rather assign the task to a dean, who may assign it to a division chair or some other appropriate person. While there are always exceptions, as a general rule a president should make sure that an assignment is a presidential assignment before accepting it.

Use Presidential Influence to Have the College Represented. In refusing an assignment, the president must not remove the college from activities or organizations with which it should be involved. When appropriate, the president should use the office to ensure that the college is represented, thereby magnifying the influence of the president and the college without committing the president to too many activities. A fringe benefit of this approach is that it provides avenues for developing the leadership skills of other members of the college community.

Address the Media as the President. Most questions from the media, other than those relating to policy, should be referred to subordinates unless the opportunity exists to make the president and therefore the college look good. Presidents should remember that by speaking on everything, they are heard on nothing, or at least very little. A president who uses the media to comment on too many trivial events uses up the presidential stance and eliminates a "fallback" position, not only for the office but for the college as well. If the president feels the media have been inaccurate in fact or in interpretation, let someone else challenge them unless a policy question is involved. As someone once said, never pick a fight with someone who buys ink by the barrel and paper by the ton.

Address the College Community as the President. Presidents are asked their opinions daily by members of the campus community. As when dealing with the media, the president who comments on a campus issue before it reaches the presidential level has all but eliminated a fallback position for the office. By entering the wrong debate or even the right debate at the wrong time, a president appears to take a stand too early in the debate. Then he or she faces the possibility of having to reverse the previous stand, thereby appearing to be indecisive, or worse yet, the possibility of climbing out on a limb, arming trustees and others with saws on the way out. Although the successful president should engage in any number of formal and informal conversations with members of the college community, he or she should always keep in mind that when speaking it is as president of the institution.

Engage in Low-Energy, High-Yield Activities. The concept of low energy, high yield will be essential to the effective presidency in the future. While the situation varies from person to person, from college to college, and from year to year, the concept is valid and should be cultivated by presidents. To illustrate, if you as president are asked to serve as chair of the United Way Campaign and you know that the organization consistently achieves its goals, has a competent staff, requires little time and work on the part of the chair, and receives a great deal of positive publicity, accept the position, for the college and the president will receive high dividends from this low-energy, high-yield activity. On the other hand, the payoff for working your way through the chairs of the Rotary, Kiwanis, and similar organizations is at best marginal, and in the final analysis is probably a high-energy, low-yield activity.

(As suggested many times in this volume, situations vary. One president of a midsized community college in a southeastern state claims that membership in the Rotary Club is critical to his success as a president, for everyone who makes decisions in town is a member of the Rotary Club. Serving as an officer is expected of leading members of the community, especially of the community college president.)

Trustees are infamous for forcing presidents into low-yield, high-energy activities (an invitation to address the ten-member American Legion Post, or whomever, on Saturday afternoon is an example). A president can deter trustees from making too many demands by projecting a presidential image that conveys the message that the president should be expected to do certain things and not others.

Beware of Leaping Monkeys.[1] Presidents have a special propensity for attracting other people's problems, and new presidents have a special talent for attracting and ultimately owning other people's monkeys. As one president acknowledges, "I am a human garbage can in terms of the absorption of problems. I suffer fools wisely and recognize that the presidency is a dumping ground as well as a provider of inspiration." Stated another way, many deans and others who report to the president are past masters at shifting monkeys—problems—from their backs onto someone else's. Faculty members, too, are experts at getting monkeys off their backs; they derive special pleasure from watching the little devils leap from one administrator to another. When faculty members are successful in passing monkeys to the president, they gleefully rush out to inform the dean or division chair that the president has *approved* their project, when all the president really said was that it sounded like a good idea and one worth pursuing. In any event, too often the back, or the desk if you wish, on which the leaping monkeys land is the president's.

To illustrate, it is a rare president indeed who has not met a faculty member or administrator in the hallway, in an office, or elsewhere and been presented with an "absolutely great idea." The president, in an attempt to show interest (which may or may not be genuine), finds the temptation to react to the idea almost irresistible. Too many times when the president is asked for a reaction the response is, "Let me think about it and get back to you." Every time the president agrees to "get back" to someone in this manner, he or she has just taken on someone else's monkey, for it is now up to the president to make the next move. Every time the dean comes into the president's office with the all-too-familiar "We've got a problem," the dean, by using we, has just passed a monkey on to the president.

By accepting someone else's problems, the president is placed in the position of subordinate and is no longer in charge of the situation, for the person passing the monkey has engaged in the act (some call it an art) of reverse delegation. One thing the president can count on is that once the monkey lands on his or her back, the original owner will stop by to ask about the progress being made in solving the problem. And no matter how well the monkey is cared for, the president will get little credit, for once the monkey is healthy and grown and adopted by the college com-

---

[1] I am indebted to William Onchen, Jr., and Donald L. Wass' "Management Time: Who's Got the Monkey?", *Harvard Business Review,* November–December 1974. The "golf course" example is taken directly from the authors, as is the analogy used in the following discussion.

munity, the original owner will point with pride to the success of his or her monkey, of his or her great idea.

One can test one's propensity to attract and own other people's monkeys. For example, after a weekend or holiday of playing "catch up" on office work, ask those who report to you what they did during their time off. If they went to the beach, the mountains, played golf, tennis, or just hung around with the family, and you worked to catch up, then too many monkeys have made the leap to your back. Or if you are rushing to the office on Saturday morning and you pass the deans on the golf course, you have problems no matter how cheerfully they wave to you as you rush by.

Stage Formal Ceremonies. Presidents should take every opportunity to establish and maintain the legitimacy of the office. The formal inauguration, which can be an important symbol of the office, should be planned with care, ensuring that the legitimate power of the presidency is bestowed by the authority that is legally authorized to grant the privileges and outline the responsibilities of the office. Symbols such as presidential medallions can be helpful in establishing a tradition and passing the tradition on to future presidents, as can formal receptions given by the president. Moreover, a formal inauguration ceremony announces to the academic community and the community at large that assuming the presidency is an important act and that the position warrants respect.

SUMMARY

Presidents can enhance the mystique surrounding the presidency and increase presidential effectiveness by resisting current expectations and working to create new expectations on the part of the faculty, the board, and the public in general. Presidents must extricate themselves from mundane campus and community affairs and place themselves in a position of speaking and acting as leaders of important educational institutions. By realizing that they cannot be all things to all people and by realizing that they not only have a right but an obligation to develop a presidential stance—a mystique—presidents can bring a focus to the position that is often lacking. The result will be happier and more effective presidents and more successful institutions.

4

HOW LONG IS TOO LONG?
The Question Presidents and Trustees Fear to Ask

Exits are almost as important as entrances but, while the latter are sometimes well staged, the former are usually improvised.
    —From *Presidents Make a Difference*, directed by Clark Kerr

Being a president is much like dancing with a big bear. You don't quit when you get tired. You quit when the bear gets tired.
    —James C. Henderson

The major threat to the presidency and therefore to the community college achieving its full potential is that too many presidents have settled comfortably into that middle ground on the presidential continuum where survival, not leadership, is the issue; where presidents are neither effective leaders nor failures; where average is the order of the day, not excellent.[1] The major threat, then, is when presidents stay in their positions

---

[1] In *The Community College Presidency*, I devoted a chapter to presidential burnout. My conclusion was and is that relatively few presidents suffer from burnout, if one defines burnout as the inability to function in a position because of mental stress. Burnout does occasionally occur among presidents, as it does among members of almost all occupations. When it occurs, the president has definitely stayed in his or her position too long, even to the point of needing medical help. But in studying the presidency, I found burnout as defined by members of the medical profession to be so rare among active community college presidents that the subject, while important and one which presidents should be familiar with and sensitive to, is not a major concern of current community college presidents.

without providing effective leadership; the major problem is when presidents stay too long. But how long is too long?

THE COMPLEXITY OF MOVING

The most important professional decision a community college administrator makes is accepting a presidency. The second most important professional decision that person makes may well be deciding when to leave a presidency. Probably no question haunts the introspective president more than the question of how long is too long to stay in one position and continue to provide effective leadership. Even the most egotistical among us begin to wonder if we are providing effective leadership after we have been in our position for a few years, no matter how well things seem to be functioning. The complexity of the question makes it especially troubling, for as one twenty-two-year veteran of the presidency notes, "Some people give all they have to a college in one year; others never run out of ideas." How long is too long? In one instance two years may be too long; in another a lifetime may not be too long.

In the same vein, the most important decision many governing boards make is the selection of a president. The second most important decision most governing boards make is getting rid of their first most important decision. As trustees evaluate the president both formally and informally, they must deal with the question of how long is too long to retain the same president. Fortunately for presidents and trustees, most of the trustees' time and energy is devoted to the overall welfare of the college rather than to employing and dismissing presidents.

Even asking the question of how long is too long is difficult, for the elusive, emotional, and troublesome answers often involve much rationalization not only on the part of the president but on the part of the board as well. Ironically, the president who is introspective enough to ask how long is too long is likely pragmatic enough to discover that few people are standing in line to employ ex-presidents. As I concluded in my earlier study of the community college presidency, for most individuals, there is no life after the presidency, at least not at the same level of prestige, salary, and excitement (Vaughan 1986, pp. 216–22). Similarly, many board members are willing to settle for a little less than they desire in a president rather than go through the often-traumatic process of dismissing one president and hiring another. Presidents who are considering changing positions fear that the next position may not be as good as the one they already have; trustees who are considering encouraging the current president to seek employment elsewhere fear that the next president might not be any better than, or even as good as, the current one. The result is often a mental, emotional, and pragmatic compromise resulting in the president staying in a position until a major crisis forces the board or the president to act. The question of how long is too long remains in the closets of the minds of presidents, trustees, and everyone else who has a vested interest in the community college presidency, for it is indeed the question that most people fear to ask.

CAN ONE TELL HOW LONG IS TOO LONG?

Can even the most perceptive president tell how long is too long to stay in one position? Are there signals the governing board should look for, when evaluating the president, that might indicate when it is time for a change? Certainly the research on the ideal length of presidential tenure is inconclusive. The Association of Governing Board's study of the presidency directed by Clark Kerr concludes that there is no ideal length of time for a president to stay in office. "We see no ideal length of term, whether five for a community college president or ten for a private liberal arts college president. It depends so much on the person and the situation of the institution" (Kerr 1984, p. 64). The study notes that it takes at least a year for a president to get established in the position and that the last year in office is not fully effective, thereby reducing the effective tenure of most presidents by two years (p. 63). James Fisher believes that "There appears to be a point of diminishing returns for most leaders—a point in time beyond which they lose effectiveness" (Fisher 1984, p. 22). For the college president, Fisher believes the maximum time for most presidents to exert effective leadership is from six to ten years. (p. 49). On the other hand, David Riesman feels that even a decade may be too little time for a president to serve if he or she wants to have an impact on the quality and collegiality of the faculty and staff. He suggests that "Perhaps spouses' judgment, for either sex, can be the most trusted verdict as to when enough is enough" (Clodius and Magrath 1984, p. 171).

In my study of the community college presidency, I touched briefly upon the subject of how long is too long for a president to occupy a position:

> For years, a favorite parlor game among presidents has been speculating on how long is too long to occupy the presidency. As in the case with most parlor games, one's perspective on the game changes with age, availability of desirable options, and the satisfaction associated with the game itself. And, indeed, as with most games, the players are not always able to control their length of office, for there are always certain rules, referees, and others who have an influence on any one career. Indeed, for the community college presidents, the board, the faculty, and any number of individuals have some say in how long the tenure may be (Vaughan 1986, p. 223).

One conclusion was that those presidents who were identified as leaders by their colleagues had been in office a median of 9.4 years versus a median of 5.3 years for all presidents, making clear that in most cases more than the proverbial 5–7 years are required to establish oneself as a leader in the field (ibid., p. 224).

While there are no written rules that say that a president's time is up, based upon correspondence and interviews with presidents and trustees, I believe that there are signals that serve to warn us that a president has been in a position too long. In most cases, ignoring the signals diminishes the president's effectiveness. Moreover, by recognizing the warning signals, presidents and trustees can take steps that will prolong and perhaps improve presidential effectiveness.

Signals

One twenty-three-year veteran of three presidencies shared the following observations with me. He found the position as the founding president of a small rural college to be a "wonderful training ground" but a position that did not sustain his drives and needs beyond the training period. When he realized that the training period was over, he moved to the presidency of a yet-to-be-opened urban college, a position he found challenging at first. After eight years in the position, he experienced a feeling "of déjà vu, of repetitiveness of problems and personalities." Eight years, if not too long, were certainly enough for him in that position.

Renewal and new challenges were sought in the chancellorship of a large urban district. He and the district weathered a number of financial crises, faculty unrest, intensified union activities, erratic enrollments, faculty retrenchment, and any number of other stressful activities that became common on community college campuses during the late 1970s and early 1980s. Moreover, he found that as chancellor he had fewer and fewer contacts with the campus and became more and more alienated from the faculty. While events took their toll, they alone were not enough to signal it was time to move on. In his third position as chief executive officer, a new factor entered into his thinking and a new way of evaluating longevity in a position wormed its way to the surface: aging. He recalls:

> The force of denial of aging is a curious one. All of us carry around in our heads a sense of self based on our youth, or early maturity. The wrinkles in our faces and in our hearts are ignored, and we pretend that we are the same as we were decades ago. But we are not, and ultimately we grope toward a personal solution to the problem of the final years of our careers and to the need to plan for them, as well as for post-retirement. As I saw age 60 looming ahead, I had to ask myself whether I wanted to be a CEO for the remainder of my life in higher education or try something else. My answer was something else.

How long is too long? For this individual in his final presidency, too long was when he felt time running out, at least professionally.

Another president relates that he was brought face-to-face somewhat by accident with the need to evaluate the desirability of moving to a new position. As the president of a rural college located far from the state capital he had to fly to the capital for meetings, often as frequently as twice a month. In order to reach his destination, it was necessary to change planes at the same airline terminal, a terminal that served over 1 million passengers a year. On one trip his spouse accompanied him for the first time on this particular route. Walking into the cocktail lounge, they located a cozy spot at the end of the bar. While still ten feet away from them, the cocktail waitress glanced in the president's direction and inquired: "The usual?" This president decided then and there that it was time to move on, for indeed he was beginning to fall into a routine in his thinking and actions, even to the extent of his travels. He admits that the incident in the airport lounge could not be directly related to his performance as president; however, it symbolically reinforced the feeling that things were becoming too routine, that he needed a change in habits and scenery, including airline terminals. In fewer than six months he left his position for the presidency of another college, this one within an hour's drive of the state capital.

Another person who had been in the presidency for over twenty years at six different colleges, ranging in tenure from eleven years to three interim presidencies of less than a year each (a hired gun or Paladin, as one Texas newspaper proclaimed upon his arrival), was preparing to leave his most recent presidency, a position he had occupied for six years, when I interviewed him. He found the question of how long is too long intriguing, for obviously my interview was not the first time he had considered the question.

While hesitating to place a time limit on a president's service at one college, he nevertheless believes that it is good for the individual and for the institution if the college changes presidents periodically. He believes that how long one should stay depends upon a number of things: one's own goals, the situation at the institution, and any number of other professional and personal factors that influence one's ability to lead and one's life beyond the position. In the final analysis, however, his instinct told him when to move.

> For me, when things feel right, this sounds astrological, but when the stars line up—those stars are institutional and personal: current institutional status, my own personal needs at the time—when they all are in alignment, it's time to make a decision and so I just make that decision and don't worry about what comes next. I wouldn't recommend this approach to everyone, for there is a vulnerability and a liability in it. You have to assume it could be difficult. Fortunately, I've come through those things all right; there is an alignment that occurs that you feel is right and you do it. And we all have those feelings. I try to act on mine when I can.

One star that was not in alignment, according to the president, was a series of recently completed negotiations with the four unions on campus, for he noted that the last round of negotiations had been very, very difficult, so much so that some bridges were burned. Did the contract negotiations convince this president that he had stayed too long? No. Did they make the decision to move easier? Yes.

A veteran trustee alludes to the personal side of the presidency as one aspect that, while difficult to control, can and does affect presidential performance. He refers to the personal side of the presidency as the human element, rather than professional. He observes:

> I don't think all of the terminations that have happened around the country are necessarily the result of a defect in a person's qualifications. Sometimes the president's personal station in life dictates attention to some matters that are unrelated to the college and demand more time and energy than the board expects or desires. There's a breakdown in communications, and I think those signs, while not easily documented, are fairly obvious, such things as when board votes become struggles and little things are problematic that should be automatic.

Another symptom of staying too long is when a president finds he or she is developing a routine in which he repeats himself to the college community and to the community at large. The routine expresses itself in a number of ways: telling the same stories to the same people, expressing the same ideas, offering the same solutions, and answering questions that have not even been asked. As one trustee notes, "Certainly when a president starts taking the college, the board, and the institution for granted, when the president becomes stale, when the president is no longer providing dynamic leadership, but is just continuing along at the same old pace doing the same old thing, then it's time to go."

The tenure in office that permits the routine to develop also creates a strange sense of ownership in the college, especially for founding presidents, but for others as well. A signal that the ownership syndrome is developing sounds when criticisms of the college are taken personally. "Why are they criticizing *my* college?" becomes a recurring question. A trustee warns:

> One of the things presidents and trustees need to watch out for is an increasingly defensive posture by the president. When presidents start feeling defensive, they need to back off and analyze what it's all about because it could be really important for their own well-being. I know from experience that getting oneself into a defensive posture doesn't enhance one's presence, self-worth, security and how one feels about the job. If up front presidents would start to recognize it when they see an increasing amount of defensiveness, then they could get a clearer picture of their

posture. Now, it doesn't mean they can't turn it around, but they can never turn it around if they don't identify it. Defensiveness is a real signal regarding how long may be too long. I see defensiveness as a move toward paranoia.

Most presidents feel at one time or another that they have every reason to be defensive. Criticisms from internal and external sources may be no more than the type of questioning that normally exists in a healthy institution. Overreaction to criticism results in a defensiveness bordering, as the trustee suggests, on paranoia. The longer one stays in a position, the more aspects of the college one has a vested interest in and thus the more things one feels defensive about. Once the president takes criticisms of the college too personally, it is perhaps time to move on. When the questions by the faculty are no longer viewed as a right and responsibility but rather as a subversive activity designed to undermine the president's "rule," the president and board should heed the warning.

One former president who admits to missing the presidency tremendously offers his observations on tenure in office. He, like others, feels that once your goals are realized, you have fulfilled your role at that particular college. He believes that once you avoid getting into the fray and everything becomes anticlimactic, your time is up, as is the case when *everyone* has heard your stories not once but several times. He feels that when you lose your patience and refuse to answer "stupid questions" from those who should know the answers, especially board members, then you may have overstayed your usefulness at that particular college. An especially dangerous warning signal, he notes, is when the president believes that he is a law unto himself, a situation that becomes extremely dangerous because it leads the president to believe he can (and should!) ignore the rules, regulations, advice, requests, and directives of the college community and governing board.

A former president who resigned after serving for a number of years simply found that his priorities had changed. "On the surface, for me, there were several logical reasons why I should exercise the options available for me to step away from my professional responsibilities and take a good look at what I wanted to do with the rest of my life." Among the logical reasons were that he was eligible for early retirement, his children had finished college and had left home, his spouse was seeking professional opportunities beyond those available in the community in which they lived, and he wanted to pursue photography as a second career.

On the other hand, there were reasons for leaving the presidency that were not so logical for this individual. As he points out, some reasons for his leaving were emotional. In his words:

> I am a person who gets ego satisfaction from doing a good job and having it appreciated and acknowledged. When I came to ———— Community College,

the place was in a shambles, and I was successful in straightening it out. Of course, in the beginning I got lots of positive feedback. After about five years though, that became history, and I started to feel that I was being taken for granted. I guess I felt I was responsible for everyone and everything, and no one seemed to consider what was happening to me. So I guess, for me, five or six years would have been long enough for maximum reward. How long is too long, how much is too much is not easy to answer. In the presidential seat some days were miserable, but I always knew a good one was going to come along. Maybe "too much" is related to the amount of time between the bad days and the good ones. Maybe too long is when one starts feeling too alone and unappreciated. There are a lot of actors in that scenario: family, board, immediate staff, colleagues. Come to think of it, I probably left the presidency for basically the same reasons I divorced my first wife. The ecstasy wasn't worth the agony, and I had another option.

One nationally recognized community college leader offers the following observations.

There is no magic number of years to stay in a position, but if pressed I believe I would pick seven. By that time you should have been able to accomplish your major goals. Also, if by then you haven't alienated enough people and groups to pose a serious threat to your continued presence, you should be fired for being too passive. But if they are about to do you in because of your cumulative "sins" you should leave under your own power before they nail you.

Most authorities on leadership agree that the effective leader has to have the support of those he or she is leading, and if the leader loses the support of any major constituency or becomes too closely aligned with any one group while ignoring others, he or she has probably stayed too long. One president identifies the danger inherent in becoming too close to any single group.

My observation is that the longer a president stays, the greater the temptation to become encapsuled with the same set of people, and a kind of clique develops. We spend more time with those with whom we've become comfortable and lose touch with other members of the faculty, staff, and community. This isolation or encapsulation can be the kiss of death. Over time, we let the psychological aspects work on us to some extent; we don't want to be in the presence of those with whom we have had intense disagreements. And so there is a dodging phenomenon that is at work. The same might be said for members of the board where there have been policy disagreements or what have you.

One veteran president warns against placing too much emphasis on satisfying a single group, even the board. He states:

It seems to me as if you cannot continue to lead without the support—a
general consenting to your leadership—of those you are supposed to lead.
Obviously, you will always make decisions people don't like, sometimes
more often than not. One of the things that bothers me when I talk with my
colleagues is their feeling that to hell with everyone else as long as the board
likes what I'm doing, that's all that's important. That's bull, pure bull.
Obviously, the board has to be in favor of what you are doing, but board
members are not the group you are trying to lead in the last instance, for it
has to be the faculty and administrators.

He concludes that if a president loses the support of any major segment
of the college community—faculty, staff, administration, or students—he
or she has stayed too long. Ironically perhaps, when presidents lose the
support of an internal group, the faculty for example, the board tends to
rally behind the president rather than question presidential leadership, at
least in the short run.

Personal and professional integrity are recurring themes in the discussion of how long one should stay in a position. One veteran of the presidency touches upon this dilemma:

If you are dedicated to the goals you've mouthed off about, don't hang in
there when you've lost your effectiveness just because you've assembled the
political guns to beat off attackers. However, don't be too noble and leave at
a bad time for you and those depending on you when you know damned well
no one else could do any better than you.

A president who just completed his tenth year in one position noted
that he had given some thought to the question concerning length of time
in a position. He believes there are certain vital signs that indicate
whether or not the president is effective in a position, irrespective of how
long he or she has served. He observes:

You are alive and well if the planning process is still vital and
comprehensive. If the planning process includes the faculty and staff, the
administration, trustees, the endowment directors, the advisory committees,
the members of the public at large, students and others in an organized
fashion, I believe the institution is healthy and vital. When faculty members,
staff, and administrators buy into a plan, they buy in because some of that
plan was their own thoughts, their own ideas, their own projections of where
the institution ought to go. The problems come when we plan without
including people who are going to be affected by the plan. I think you are
alive and well if the board never gets around to mentioning your contract to
you. Some presidents have contracts—I don't. But if the very concept of
contract is on the tip of the tongues of people who are the movers and
shakers, then I think the president is in trouble. But you are dead in the
water if trustees seem evasive about contract length or if there hasn't been a
contract, and they begin to mention that maybe we need a contract. I think
you are alive and well if the faculty and staff never mention how long your

predecessor served. Some people will go around to the back door to let you know that you've probably stayed too long or long enough and use the predecessor's tenure as a kind of benchmark. You're dead in the water if people ask questions such as when you will be moving up to a larger school.

There are many psychological and physical aspects to the question of how long is too long, some of which are related to aspects of physical and mental aging. As one president notes, "If a president finds that it is easier not to take on new projects, not to travel to meetings, not to attend seminars and participate in other forms of renewal because he or she feels that all that can be learned has been learned, the end is near." The president who quits learning, who no longer finds excitement in the presidency, will find that the ability to inspire others becomes more difficult and occurs less frequently, thereby diminishing the president's effectiveness.

Leaving the presidency after a number of years, one president found himself enjoying a feeling of freedom that he had not experienced for years.

> If anything, I have gotten off my own case. . . . I am happier about myself than I have been for a long time, at least 25 years. My stress card now usually registers blue, a reversal of the black response I was getting a year ago. I am certain that I have taken myself, my job, my relationships too seriously in the past. It is much easier now for me just to let things be . . . and everything seems to turn out just as well as when I was working hard at it.

As every president is aware, the psychological aspects of the position spill over into family life. Family pressures push one to stay too long (or in some cases, to leave too early), as do financial considerations. In the words of one president,

> There are some things that occur which force presidents to stay beyond the time they feel they should leave. And we all have those pressures—you know, kids in school and those kinds of things we are all confronted with and I wouldn't belittle that because they are powerful forces in our lives. I have a teenager and I have to cope with that. I don't have a wife now; that was one of the prices I paid for the presidency, as have others. But anyway, there are those kinds of things. I know a lot of us are just killed by the presidency, because these roles have to have some imagination, some creativity, and when we stay too long I think we feel stultified, and if the creativity and imagination are cut off, it's just one more year, one more year, one more year.

A Tentative Checklist

Any checklist used to gauge presidential effectiveness is at best tentative and subjective. With this disclaimer in mind, the following list should provide some guidance for presidents and trustees in dealing with the elusive but important question of how long is too long for a president to remain in a position.

When Nothing Is Exciting. Based upon many discussions with presidents and trustees, the single most important factor in deciding when one should move on is when there is no more excitement, when, as one trustee observes, "presidents who have lost their enthusiasm for the job become kind of sour and a devil-may-care attitude develops." Individuals express themselves in different ways and at different stages of their career on this topic: I find the job is no longer fun; I find that nothing about the presidency excites me any more; I find everything about the position boring; I no longer want to go to work on Monday morning and I want to leave work at noon on Friday; I no longer feel creative; I have no energy, although I am physically healthy; I no longer want to talk to faculty or students; I dread board meetings, no matter what good news I have to share; I no longer get any highs from being president. The list goes on, depending upon how the person doing the talking chooses to express a lack of enthusiasm for the position. In the words of a trustee,

> If the unhappiness outweighs the happiness at some point, obviously that's going to be transmitted in all that we do in the job. Other people are going to pick up that there's less intensity, less spirit, less enthusiasm, so that drive and commitment to implement the mission and do what's right for the institution is diminished.

No matter how one expresses it, the conclusion is the same: once the excitement for the position is missing, the president has stayed too long.

When Everything Must Be Exciting. Ironically, the loss of excitement is only one side of the coin. The opposite of a loss of enthusiasm is when a president reaches a stage when every day must provide new highs in excitement, accomplishments, and challenges. A day that offers no highs is more than boring; it is frustrating and viewed by the president as "nonproductive." A day without highs leaves the president edgy and with a sense of emptiness, even failure. A day that other presidents long for leaves these presidents waiting for the next day's mail or the next trip out of town. These presidents like to ride the roller coaster, but they find the depths of the ride and the climb to the top depressing. They are often exciting individuals, but their lust for excitement is hard to sustain. They tend to be both physically and mentally tough, a toughness often forged in almost endless intellectual battles either with their colleagues or themselves. They can survive for years in the presidency, assuming their own minds and bodies can adjust, for their energy, curiosity, drive, and force of personality sustain them, although they may not give 100 percent of their efforts to the position. Neither the governing board nor members of the college community detect any large number of signals that these presidents have been in the position too long, for these presidents give off few signals that can be detected by others. The conclusion is that only these presidents themselves, and perhaps their spouses, know when it is time to move on.

When Priorities Cannot Be Established. The failure of the president to establish priorities can create a number of problems for the president and the college, in part because this failure is highly visible and subject to the evaluation of much of the college community and especially to administrators who work directly with the president. When everything becomes equally important, everything becomes routine, and the temptation is to do those things that require the least effort, especially intellectual effort. The result is something of an academic Gresham's law, with relatively unimportant tasks remaining in circulation and important tasks requiring high intellectual energy being put in abeyance. When the president can no longer establish priorities, it is time for that individual to seek a new position and time for the board to seek a new president.

When the Agenda Is Completed. Most presidents have certain goals they wish to accomplish upon assuming the presidency. Several presidents stated their belief that it is time to move on when one's goals have been accomplished. Unless one publicly outlines very specific goals upon assuming the presidency, only the incumbent can say that the agenda is complete. Stated another way, only the president can say when the stars are in alignment, to use the example discussed above, and therefore it is time to move on. When the president believes that the agenda is completed (no matter how much of the agenda is fabricated over the years), then it is time to move on, regardless of the perception of others.

When Lower Standards Are Accepted. As suggested in Chapter 1, presidents are responsible for setting the campus climate, which includes establishing institutional standards. A danger signal occurs when presidents start to let the little things slip. Such things as ignoring a less-than-clean building, grass that has gone a week too long without mowing, letters with a "small typo," and personnel who are just a "little late" are symptoms of a bigger problem. Once a president accepts lower standards in small things, it is just a matter of time until he accepts lower standards in grading, recruitment of faculty, and other matters that go to the very heart of the institution. Most presidents mellow with age and experience; however, when standards that were once unacceptable are ignored, the president may well have stayed too long.

When the Vote Is One of No Confidence. When a governing board casts a vote of no confidence in the president, he has obviously stayed in the position too long. Or if the president has alienated the governor's office or powerful members of the state legislature, he or she is usually forced out. On the other hand, if the faculty casts a vote of no confidence in the president, it may not be so obvious to everyone that he or she has stayed in the position too long. Indeed, as suggested earlier, board members often rally behind presidents in whom the faculty has cast a vote of no confidence, thereby creating the impression that these presidents are still viable leaders. Although circumstances vary greatly, and some faculty may give the president a vote of no confidence for failing to deal effectively with events well beyond his or her control, the rule of thumb should be that if the president loses the confidence of a major segment of the college community, he or she has been in the position too long. A trustee, in discussing a lack of confidence in the president, sums up the situation as follows: "When there's a division of the ways—when the president is backed into a corner by the faculty, the union, or some other segment of the community—unless he has a method and a mode of successfully working out, I think the time has come that he should look for another job and there should be a fresh start at the college."

When the Fit Is No Longer Right. The combinations of things that go into making the effective leader are many, elusive, and varied. One of the intangible ingredients in the leadership formula is what some people refer to as chemistry, or "fit." As many presidents and trustees have discovered, the fit may be right when a president first assumes a position and may later become so incompatible as to make the position unbearable. Why? Circumstances change; presidents change (as noted in one of the examples above, that first rural college presidency that provided so much excitement in the beginning of a presidential career was no longer a good fit after a few years); faculties change; administrators change; and most importantly, boards change, especially in community colleges. Board members who employ a president have a vested interest in his or her success; subsequent board members have less of a vested interest.

Speaking of the proper fit, the chemistry that goes to make up the successful presidency, a trustee and former president of the Association of Community College Trustees board of directors made the following comments:

> It seems to me that if the chemistry is right at the time of hiring, people of good professional status will recognize when it's wrong. And somehow or other, when trustees change, some of the chemistry is lost because the president is not working with the same group of people, but that understanding has to be translated to those trustees who replace those who made the decision to hire the president in the first place. But obviously people of different talents fit different circumstances at different times; it just seems to me that there's got to be a chemistry between that president and the new board, and when it's lost, they ought to both recognize it and do something about it.

Community colleges boards are made up entirely of local citizens, have a relatively small number of members and short terms of office, are subject to the ebb and flow of local politics, and are often elected. As a result of these circumstances, community college boards are especially vulnerable to a change in makeup, in chemistry. When the chemistry changes between the board and the president, when the fit is no longer right, it is time for the president to move along. As one president observes, the fit is no longer right when the president not only cannot answer questions from the board but resents their even being asked. Or, as a trustee phrases it, "The fit may be right at the beginning, you know. A human being has only so many ideas, so many new thoughts; you do something for a period of time, and it becomes kind of old hat. That's when it's time for the president to go." Presidents who realize that the chemistry is no longer right may well head off a vote of no confidence or a dismissal if they move on their own.

When No Risks Are Taken. Presidents who always lean toward safe decisions no longer challenge the college community or themselves. Risk-taking is generally accepted by most experts on leadership as a characteristic of the leader. Always playing it safe brings the seesaw to a halt, to refer to the metaphor used earlier. Presidents who are no longer willing to put their reputation, indeed their career, on the line for what they believe is right have become too comfortable (or too insecure) and should move on.

When "They" Want You. A consultant on presidential searches reminded a group of fifty presidents attending a summer workshop in Vail, Colorado, that the dagger is always pointed at the heart of the president and that the board always has at least one dagger in its arsenal. In his opinion, all the board has to do is get a study going and then point out that the study has certain holes, or that the president is not doing what the study suggests; therefore, the board is not pleased and must seriously examine the president's performance. One president puts it more succinctly: "If they want you, they will get you." He suggests that you can substitute almost any group for the board—the faculty, other administrators, the public—and come up with the same answer. If they want you, you are gone, especially if "they" are the governing board, the governor, or key members of the state legislature.

When the President "Self-Destructs." Cohen and March believe that presidents who are preparing to leave the position develop "cooling-out" strategies. They note:

> Presidents will behave so as to make the job unpleasant in ways that do not detract from their basic subjective perception of success in it. We would expect them to make themselves intolerably busy—and increasingly so as

they approach resignation. They would see the demands on them as increasingly conflictual—and make them so—particularly as they come closer to the time for resignation. They grow tired and sick. (1974, p. 193)

Cohen and March's cooling-out hypothesis bears serious consideration when a president is deciding if he or she has been in a position too long. When presidents find that they are looking for reasons to leave—lowering aspirations, to use Burton Clark's term—they have been in the position too long. One trustee, while not using the term "cooling out" and not being familiar with the Cohen and March hypothesis, believes that those presidents who decide to leave react in much the same way as Cohen and March describe. He observes:

I have yet to see a president who announced a retirement to come in a year or two who didn't fall off rather dramatically. I've hated to see it happen, but I've seen it in almost every case I can think of. It's just human nature, what's the old word—figmo. The attitude is, "I've done it, I've had it, I'm going out in a year or so," and it just tails off. I've seen boards buy a president to retain him an extra year. Boards have done that to their own dissatisfaction.

When the Seesaw Stops. Chapter 1 depicted the president atop the seesaw as a way of metaphorically describing the position. The discussion suggested that the greatest danger to the college comes when the seesaw stops. A trustee captures the essence of the argument in a brief statement:

Sometimes there's not an unhappiness and not a defensiveness, but the contented nature of both the board and the president to accept the status quo is very dangerous and important to the college. I doubt that the contented president and the contented board have the ability to recognize that they're so contented that they're not moving. They're willing to lie down and go to sleep. But things probably seem to be going rather smoothly, but I doubt that they're serving the community as well as they might.

When the seesaw stops, it is time for the president to move on.

When the Grass Is Greener. Most presidents are tempted at various stages of their careers to seek other positions: a larger college, a professorship, a position with business and industry, all at times seem to offer more prestige, more challenge, and more money than one's current position. Once the incumbent receives an offer or even imagines that positions are available for the taking, it is difficult to be satisfied and fully productive in the current position. When the president reaches the stage that he or she believes the grass is greener in someone's else's field, it is time to move on.

One could point to other warning signals that may indicate that a president has been in a position too long. Many of the obvious reasons, such as breaking the law or the rules and regulations of the governing board, are not discussed here. Nor is out-and-out incompetence discussed. One assumes that in the case of character flaws or incompetence the president has stayed too long and practically everyone realizes that. What has been presented here are the more subtle warning signals that often go unheeded or are not acted upon by either the board or the president. In almost every instance, some of these signals are present in those situations where the presidents are not performing to their own satisfaction, to the satisfaction of the board, the college community, or the community at large. Presidents and trustees can use the above signals as a means of sensitizing themselves to when a president has stayed too long. With some forethought, the signals can be dealt with early and often in a positive way, thereby saving a great deal of grief for all concerned and perhaps saving a president from being reminded that he or she has stayed too long.

PROLONGING PRESIDENTIAL EFFECTIVENESS

The foregoing, if taken in isolation, presents a somewhat gloomy picture regarding the community college presidency. While the presidency is not without its pitfalls, its overall prospects are far from gloomy. Indeed, most community college presidents are quite happy in their position (Vaughan 1986, pp. 3; 45–46; 99; 100–2). All of the above, with the possible exception of a vote of no confidence, are personal in the sense that the president, rather than an outside force, controls most of the circumstances. Personal mistakes are difficult to deal with if for no other reason that they are hard for one to see and understand. I believe, however, that some steps can be taken to prolong presidential effectiveness.

(1) Presidents should prepare intellectually and psychologically for life after the presidency. The average tenure for a community college president is 7.2 years; over 50 percent of presidents have been in their current position for 5 years or less. The average age of current presidents is 50.7 years (ibid., pp. 209–11). In spite of these figures, most presidents approach the presidency much as they approach life, as if it will continue forever. How one prepares for life after the presidency is a story in itself and goes well beyond the limits of this chapter; however, presidents should realize that their tenure in office will likely end well before retirement.

(2) Presidents should realize that while their problems are often personal, they are not unique. Presidents in trouble should call other presidents to see how they have handled a particular problem or situation, either professional or personal. For example, rare indeed is the president

who has not found certain aspects of the presidency boring at one time or another. What do other presidents do in this case? Some take sabbaticals; others take on new projects. Most suffer in silence. National and state organizations should consider establishing a "presidential hot line" to provide a forum and advice for presidents in trouble. A presidential hot line, staffed by successful veteran presidents and in some cases trustees, could prove invaluable to new presidents and to presidents in trouble.

(3) A forum should be provided for spouses of presidents. Spouses seem amazed to find out that the problems associated with the presidency are not unique to their spouses. If spouses could get together to discuss problems and issues more often, they in turn would better understand the problems associated with the presidency and therefore could help presidents solve certain problems and cope with those they cannot solve. The spouses' forum could provide an excellent avenue for exposing the increasing number of male spouses to the presidency.

(4) Presidents should spend more time on introspection. It is important to know what the presidency is and is not; it is important to know what the president should do and should not do. Socrates' admonition that the unexamined life is not worth living is still valid. The same would seem to apply to the presidency.

(5) As suggested in Chapter 1 and in line with the above recommendation, the president should be a scholar. Some of the president's scholarship should be devoted to the study of the presidency, for much can be learned from studying the college and university presidency. By bringing a disciplined approach to introspection, the president can place problems, issues, frustrations, and other aspects of the shadow side of the presidency into perspective. Moreover, by viewing the presidency through a broader perspective, the president can bring new approaches and new understandings to the position, thereby prolonging effective leadership.

(6) Presidents and board members must discuss the presidency both philosophically and practically. The Association of Community College Trustees and the Association of Governing Boards provide excellent forums for this discussion; however, most presidents and many trustees do not use the forum. Board members are responsible for the welfare of the president, at least indirectly. Candid discussion between presidents and trustees can alleviate many of the potential problems discussed above.

(7) Finally, presidents should realize that most faculty, staff, administrators, students, and members of the public expect and want the president to lead. When the president is exercising dynamic leadership, few people, including the president, will ask how long is too long. While ultimately leadership is based on results, leadership is also a state of mind—a perceived self-confidence, to use James Fisher's term—that places presidents in charge of not only the college's destiny but their own as well. When presidents realize that leadership is desired among all constituents, many of the concerns outlined above disappear.

CONCLUSIONS

The following conclusions have been reached regarding evaluating presidential tenure. (1) Presidents and board members should devote more time and energy to the question of how long a president can occupy a presidency and continue to provide effective leadership. (2) There is no magic number of years for providing effective leadership; community colleges are as different in their presidents, needs, constituents, life cycles, and the idiosyncrasies of their boards as are other institutions of higher education. (3) Determining how long is too long is often a very sensitive, subtle, subjective process that requires honesty on the part of presidents ("It's hard, I think, for us to face up and be true to ourselves sometimes, even when we've got some very clear signals," observes a trustee) and members of the board. As suggested earlier, it is often easier in the short run for the board to stay with a less-than-desirable president and for the president to stay with a less-than-desirable presidency simply because it is traumatic to change leadership. It is also expensive and something of a gamble to change presidents. (4) A checklist should be developed to determine if a president is losing his or her effectiveness as a leader. (5) Once the checklist is developed, steps can be taken by both the board and the president to prolong the effectiveness of the president. After all, presidential effectiveness is ultimately what the board-president relationship must achieve; otherwise, both parties in the relationship are failures.

INTRODUCTION TO CHAPTERS 5 AND 6

At critical points in my life and in my academic career, mentors have given me the confidence and support without which it would have been almost impossible to carry on. Unfortunately, not everyone is so fortunate. Minority students, who perhaps need that sort of support more than most other students, often find it unavailable.

>—Walter E. Massey, professor of physics and vice president for research at the University of Chicago and director of the Argonne National Laboratory

I shouldn't say this—the women won't like me to say it—but I never thought of needing role models who were women. I never considered that I was a woman and then a scientist. My role models didn't have to be women—they could be scientists.

>—Gertrude B. Elion, winner of the 1988 Nobel Prize in Medicine

Chapters 5 and 6 are devoted to a discussion of female, black, and Hispanic presidents. Women, blacks, and ethnic minority presidents are important to the community colleges not only for what they bring to the presidency as individuals but also as symbols for others of similar background who aspire to the presidency. Women constitute 7.6 percent of all community college presidents, blacks 3.9 percent, and Hispanics 2.1 percent (Green 1988, p. 6). While female presidents are discussed in Chapter 5 and blacks and Hispanics in Chapter 6, these presidents have some things in common that they do not have in common with white male presidents.

The community college has opened the doors of higher education for many millions of female and minority students; currently female students outnumber males on most community college campuses, and on a number of campuses, blacks and Hispanics outnumber whites. The community college has indeed been a door of opportunity for those Americans who have, for much of the nation's history, found it difficult, if not impossible, to attend an institution of higher education. Has the community college's door opened as widely for women and racial minorities who aspire to be community college presidents as it has for students? Today, as has been true throughout the community college's history, the large majority of presidents are white (93 percent) and 92.4 percent are males (ibid., pp. 4, 6). However, female, black, and Hispanic presidents do constitute an important segment of the leadership of the nation's community colleges. The following chapters examine the community college presidency from the perspective of women, blacks, and Hispanics.

DEFINING PRESIDENTS

One problem in examining the community college presidency is that it is difficult to determine just who is a president, since different states and college districts define the position differently. For the purpose of this study, anyone was considered to be a president who is listed in the American Association of Community and Junior College's (AACJC) *Community, Junior, and Technical College Directory* as a president, chancellor, or director of a public two-year institution of higher education.

The lists of female, black, and Hispanic presidents were obtained from the following affiliate councils of the AACJC: the National Council of Black American Affairs; the American Association of Women in Community and Junior Colleges; and the National Community College Hispanic Council. The councils provided an identified group of female and minority presidents to survey. Since councils do not exist for other minority community college presidents who constitute approximately 1 percent (ibid., p. 6) of the community college presidential population, minorities such as Asians and American Indians were not surveyed.

The Survey

The female, black, and Hispanic presidents surveyed used the same questionnaire; only the name was changed for each of the three groups surveyed—that is, from woman to black to Hispanic. Much of the analysis in the following two chapters is based on the results of the surveys. In certain categories, the backgrounds of women, blacks, and Hispanics are compared with the backgrounds of all community college presidents as discussed in my 1986 volume, *The Community College Presidency.*

INTRODUCTORY CONCLUSIONS

Understanding the community college presidency is a complicated process, especially when one attempts to understand not only the position but how society has affected those who aspire to the office and become presidents. The female, black, and Hispanic presidents, while facing the same challenges and dilemmas confronted by other presidents, face additional dilemmas and challenges because of their race, ethnic background and sex. The following introductory conclusions offer some insights into what it means to be a minority president in today's society.

1. Stereotypes associated with women and blacks continue to cause some members of these groups difficulties in obtaining and filling the presidency. Stereotyping seems to be less of a problem with Hispanic presidents than with women and black presidents, perhaps in part because of the relatively small number of Hispanic presidents and because the majority of the Hispanic population is concentrated in a relatively small number of states.

2. A "double standard" is applied to women, blacks, and Hispanic presidents in some instances whereby they are expected to do more and be forgiven less for mistakes than is the case with white male presidents.

3. Breaking into the "good old boy" network is a major challenge for women, blacks, and Hispanics. Neither women, blacks, nor Hispanics have been able to establish peer networks that are as influential as the existing predominantly white male networks.

4. Blacks face a major problem in that they are seen as well suited to lead inner-city, predominantly black institutions but not predominantly white suburban ones.

5. Questions relating to sex are more common in the presidential interview than are questions relating to race.

6. There are assets and liabilities associated with being a female, black, or Hispanic president. In the case of women, most of the assets and liabilities are associated with "female characteristics" and therefore do not limit women to a certain type of institution. In the case of blacks, most of the assets center around being able to identify with and deal with minorities, assets that tend to limit their choice of presidencies. Hispanics tend to find fewer assets and liabilities associated with being a president than do women or blacks.

7. Fifty-four percent of the women, 54 percent of the blacks, and 10 percent of the Hispanics stated that affirmative action programs aided them in becoming president. The major contribution of affirmative action as far as the community college presidency is concerned has been to sensitize the larger society and governing boards to the assets of the minority and female presidents and to set the stage whereby women and racial and ethnic minorities are included in the pool of presidential applicants. In some few cases, affirmative action had dictated that a black fill a presidency. Hispanics are not the "target" of affirmative action programs to the extent that blacks and women are.

8. Mentors and role models are important to a number of women and minority presidents. Mentors tend to be white males; role models tend to come from the sex, race, or ethnic background of the minority president, implying that when given a choice, as in the case of role models, women and minority presidents will choose "one of their own."

9. A large number of women and minority presidents had "negative role models." The "negative role model" mentioned most often was a community college president.

10. Sixty-six percent of the female presidents view the presidency as

asexual once they assume office. Sixty percent of the Hispanic presidents see the presidency as "aracial" (the term, as used here, includes Hispanic ethnic minorities as well as blacks) once they assume office. In contrast, 69 percent of the black presidents do not see the presidency as being "aracial" once they assume office.

11. The role of the spouse was not an important factor in the selection of women or minority presidents. In no instance was the spouse a part of the interview process when blacks or Hispanics were being interviewed for the presidency. In the case of women, some questions ("Is your husband willing to move?" "Will he object to your becoming a president?") were asked regarding the spouse; however, the questions did not relate to the spouse as a member of the presidential team.

12. Racial and ethnic minorities and women face special challenges as they strive to move into the presidency. Governing boards, current presidents, the college community, and society in general remain somewhat insensitive to these challenges. However, most boards appear to want the presidency to be filled by outstanding leaders, regardless of sex, race, or ethnic background.

5

WOMEN WHO ARE PRESIDENTS

The University of Central Florida announces "Financial Management for Women in Higher Education," March 21–23, 1988 Orlando, Florida

Women are not taken seriously, especially in traditional "male" areas such as construction and finance.
       —A female community college president

Fifty-eight female presidents were surveyed; 35 returned the completed survey, for a response rate of slightly over 60 percent. Women from 17 states responded to the survey; 9 (26 percent) of the presidents responding were from California; 4 (11 percent) were from Michigan and 4 (11 percent) from Minnesota; 3 (9 percent) were from Florida; 2 presidents (6 percent) responded from Washington and two (6 percent) from Wisconsin. One respondent (each respondent represents 3 percent of the total responses) was from each of the following states: Alabama, Arkansas, Arizona, Hawaii, Massachusetts, North Carolina, New Jersey, New York, Tennessee, Texas, and West Virginia.

PATHWAY TO THE PRESIDENCY

A number of the women identified society's stereotypical picture of women as a prominent obstacle on their pathway to the presidency. One source addresses the stereotyping that women face when they aspire to positions of leadership:

> Women who wished to be leaders needed to be *extremely well qualified,* have proven records of accomplishment, and be overprepared for their positions. While these extra demands on women have somewhat dissipated over the years, strong vestiges remain today. These expectations have caused many women to overprepare, doubt themselves, and limit their aspirations. (Shavlik and Touchton 1988, p. 101)

The women responding to the survey alluded to similar stereotyping that they had to overcome. "Could a woman be strong enough to 'control' the faculty?" and "How can a woman get along in a man's world?" were two questions asked of women presidential candidates during the interview. One president spoke of a perception that women are unable to manage a budget, and another woman president notes that "they are not taken seriously, especially in traditional 'male' areas such as construction and finance." Another believes that, prior to her selection as president, "there was a question among the trustees as to whether or not I was tough enough." (She included a parenthetical statement: "I am!") One woman felt that "because of my size and sex, there was the feeling that I wasn't tough enough." The "tough syndrome" caused difficulties for yet another woman seeking the presidency. A major problem was "being accepted by the trustees' interview committee, for the consultant to the committee reported to me that 'you were viewed as not being tough enough.' I feel this perception was based on the female physical appearance because I am trained to do the job." Another female president believes that she was not considered a serious candidate for promotion to the presidency at first solely because she was a woman. Just as damaging, one felt that some men did not perceive that a woman could be competent.

Reflecting upon her interview for the presidency, a successful candidate remembers that the "questions I was asked led me to believe that qualities more common to men were preferred." One candidate perceived that trustees were nervous interviewing a woman; another felt that being a woman is a liability because people are more accustomed to dealing with men. And another saw being a woman as a liability because women are not initially taken seriously; indeed, she thought that she was "an affirmative action candidate."

The infamous "old boys' network" reared its sometimes-ugly head as a barrier for some women on their way to the presidency. One female president found becoming a part of the network to be very difficult. Another, a black, feels that being both a woman and a minority member were major obstacles to obtaining the presidency. She also notes that "men didn't help." A white woman experienced the same sense of alienation from certain men, for she felt that "male CEOs' attitudes toward women" were obstacles she had to overcome. Another found "breaking into the network of good old boys" to be a very difficult task. Not being "one of the boys" caused yet another individual to be left out of many things, even after she became president. One president noted that it was difficult for her to be accepted into the "network" because "no other woman in the state had held this type of position."

In at least one instance, not being a "good old boy" worked to one woman's advantage. She analyzed the situation this way: "The district had had a bad experience with the previous president, who was a male. There was considerable scandal in the community. I feel that the governing board felt that [as a woman] I would be a safer president because I wouldn't get into his kind of trouble."

Some of the women experienced subtle forms of discrimination. A number of women commented on the difficulty they had getting their first administrative position (coordinator-division chair), an obstacle encountered by both men and women but one that often presents special problems for women. For example, one future president found sex discrimination in her early administrative career when she often did her job without the status, title, or salary that should have accompanied the assignments and which probably would have gone to a man were he performing similar assignments. Another received a similar message, for she states that she "spent more time in the 'trenches' than men did." One respondent noted that it probably takes a woman longer to prove herself than a man. A lack of outside support that is often afforded men (from wife, family, and friends) was noted by one respondent; the situation dampened her personal aspirations for a number of years. Similarly, another woman feels that she lacked support as early as high school and was discouraged from pursuing "high aspirations." Later in life she experienced two delays that reinforced the difficulties encountered by women aspiring to be top administrators: she took time out of her career to have children, and the mobility of her spouse's career prevented her for a number of years from establishing a career pattern that would lead to the presidency. One respondent commented on the difficulties of motherhood in relationship to her move into the presidency: "The interrupted career that most women experience in their lives because of child rearing, etc. can be difficult."

The Interview

Do governing boards ask questions related to the sex of the applicant? Eight of the thirty-five respondents (almost 23 percent) stated that they had been asked one or more questions related to their gender while being interviewed for their current position. (One respondent, who had been interviewed for a dean of student services position during the early 1970s, was told by the chancellor that "he could not have a woman in the position because students are 'rough,' and they 'swear.' ") Although the number of applicants being asked such questions was relatively small and several of the questions appear to be nonsexist *unless* placed in the context of how they would sound were they asked of male applicants, the questions asked the female candidates illustrate the double standard that some women face. For example, one female applicant was asked her age and marital status, questions that would rarely if ever be asked of a male applicant. Yet, when questions of this nature are asked of women, they may be interpreted as having sexist overtones. Discussing the questions here places them in the perspective of the community college presidency and should sensitize governing boards to some of the flaws in the interview process, perhaps eliminating sex-related questions in some instances. Similarly, future female presidential candidates should be prepared to deal with such questions directly and unemotionally.

One presidential candidate was asked during the interview if she were a feminist. Another was asked if she believed in equal rights for women. Three candidates were asked questions relating to their spouses: a board member wanted to know what a candidate's husband planned to do about his job should she be selected for the presidency; another board member asked if an applicant's husband would be interested in moving into the area; and the third candidate was asked if her husband approved of her seeking the presidency.

One applicant who replaced a founding male president in a rural area in the South was asked six questions relating to her gender, including one that asked if being a woman affected her management style. Another woman was asked about her divorce a decade earlier and about the status of her current marriage. "You really don't need this job because your husband makes a good living," was the analysis given by one board member to a female applicant. Another was asked what she would do about child care for *her* children. "In your experiences have you known individuals who complained about reporting to a woman?" queried one trustee of a female candidate he was interviewing. The same candidate noted that the "interview committee discussed in front of me whether the community was 'ready' for a female president." Another was asked how she would handle men with senior status who would report to her.

As is the case with most community college presidential interviews, the spouse of the candidate was not interviewed (Vaughan 1986, pp. 159–61; Vaughan and Associates 1987, p. 96). Those questions regarding the role of the spouse—(negative questions when viewed from the perspective of a presidential applicant)—centered around the issues discussed above. The questions relate more to the perceived role of men and women in society than to the role the spouse would play as a part of the presidential team.

ASSETS AND LIABILITIES

What are the assets and liabilities associated with being a female candidate for the presidency? Are the lines clear enough to determine whether being a woman is an advantage or disadvantage? Are women rejected because of their sex? Or are women included in the pool of applications for the presidency because of their sex? The answers are far from clear. For example, one woman president states that she was interviewed for the presidency twenty times before being selected. She believes it took her so long to be selected because she was a woman. On the other hand, one could argue that she reached the interview stage so often because she was a woman. While most cases are not this extreme, this woman's experience points out the complexities of determining the role of gender in the presidential selection process.

Was being a female applicant a factor in the presidential selection process? Nineteen female presidents (slightly over 54 percent) responded that being a woman was neither an asset nor a liability; two saw being a female candidate as both an asset and liability; five saw it as a liability; and eight saw it as an asset. These responses perhaps confuse the issue of whether there are advantages or disadvantages associated with being a female applicant for the community college presidency when women are viewed as a group. Nevertheless, the individual observations of female presidents provide interesting insights into the presidential selection process and should help guide governing boards in their deliberations.

Perceived Liabilities

Thirteen of the respondents (slightly over 37 percent) stated that they had been turned down for a presidency before being selected for one. While I am not familiar with any statistics on how many attempts are required before someone successfully competes for a community college presidency, it is not unusual for applicants to apply for a number of vacancies and to be interviewed several times before being selected. (See Vaughan 1986, pp. 27–50, for a discussion of attaining the presidency). Based upon my discussions with a number of male presidents who had been interviewed for the position four or five times before being selected, it is likely that the women responding to the survey did just as well in this regard as their male colleagues. Nevertheless, nine of the thirteen believe that being a female candidate played a role in their not getting the position.[1]

Two of the women who were turned down felt intuitively that they did not get the position because they were women. Two others state without equivocation that they were turned down because they were women, al-

[1]Only five of the women responding to the survey saw being a female candidate as a liability; two saw it as being both an asset and liability. Yet nine of the respondents believe that being a woman was a factor in their not being offered a presidency in previous attempts at obtaining one. The figures would appear to be inconsistent; however, being a woman may well cause someone to lose a given position yet not be a liability in the long run. The governing board could have numerous reasons for not selecting a particular candidate; however, the nine female presidents perceive that they were rejected because of their gender.

though one who had applied for a four-year college presidency may have been perceived as being unsuitable for the position because her experiences were in a community college. One woman stated: "Yes, definitely. One trustee (a black male) told me that this was precisely the reason. They felt a man would be 'tougher' and that I might be 'eaten alive'." Another stated: "Certainly, I was told so. I interviewed as a finalist (one of two) for a four-year woman's college. They had only had male presidents. I lost on a split board vote."

Another problem faced by some women on their pathway to the presidency was marriage to a successful man. While commuter marriages are common today, the idea of the woman being the "moving force" in a family can still be disturbing to some members of society, including governing boards of colleges. Three women presidents felt that being married to successful men caused them some problems in their move to the presidency. In one case, the governing board doubted that the woman was serious in her pursuit of the presidency because her husband was employed at a university some distance from the community college. Another found that her spouse's career required that she move so frequently that it was very difficult to establish herself as a serious contender for the presidency. A third woman found that being married to a successful man hurt her career, for she was told at one time in her career "to stay home and take care of the house." (One wonders if she would have gotten the same advice had the husband not been a success and had the family needed a second income.) While these three presidents' experiences (all three are currently married) reflect a major problem for some women who aspire to the presidency, a positive sign is that of the twenty married women answering the survey, only these three reported that the spouse's career presented any difficulty for them in achieving their career goals. While the survey did not ask if the spouse had been an asset in achieving the presidency, at least one female president gives her husband a great deal of credit. Marilyn Schlack, president of Kalamazoo Valley Community College, believes "I am probably sitting in the office of the president of KVCC because of my husband. . . . He knew I was ready and he takes great pride in what I'm doing. If I had to say who was my mentor, my confidant, it's Larry Schlack" ("Marilyn Schlack," *Encore: Magazine of the Arts,* September–October 1987, p. 10).

Perceived Assets

Eight candidates perceived being a female candidate as an asset. One felt that as a woman she had only one way to go—up—a conclusion that inspired her. One white candidate noted that the state in which she worked was placed "under the gun" by the federal government to hire minorities; however, since she would be the only female president in the state, she felt it was acceptable to employ her rather than a member of a racial or ethnic minority. One respondent believes that the search committee was more attentive and perhaps more critical because she was a woman. Another felt that "being a woman and not being very self-conscious of that fact was definitely an asset." One successful candidate points out that the committee had interviewed nine men before selecting her, and she "provided some comic relief" to what had become a somewhat dreary situation. Another, in a similar vein, notes that being a female candidate was "perhaps a slight asset, in that it clearly differentiated me from my predecessor and from other applicants." Yet another believes that being a woman was an asset because she had a "sensitivity to the type of questions asked and to the concerns of the person asking the question."

The female presidents responding to the survey believe that they got to the presidency primarily because of their qualifications and ability, not because they were women. Indeed, with two exceptions[2], the nine current presidents who had previously been turned down for a presidency offered little evidence to show that being a woman was a major factor in the decision not to offer them the position. Nevertheless, the female presidents' responses suggest that some members of society still see women as stereotypes possessing "female characteristics" unsuited to the presidency. And one must keep in mind that the comments regarding stereotyping come from women who are winners in the presidential sweepstakes; those who have not had the opportunity to apply for the presidency or those who have applied and not made it would likely be much harsher in their comments. As one source cautions in alluding to the gains women have made in leadership positions, "They [women's successes] also do not tell the stories of the countless women leaders who have not been given an opportunity to serve when they were clearly ready and more than able" (Shavlik and Touchton 1988, p. 98).

Are those female presidents who feel that being a woman presents certain difficulties in obtaining the presidency and performing the duties of the office rationalizing for their own shortcomings? One would assume and hope that a certain amount of healthy rationalization takes place

[2]In reality, there was probably only one exception, for the candidate for the four-year presidency was likely turned down because she was attempting to move from a two-year vice presidency to a four-year presidency. While data on moving from a two-year to a four-year presidency are scarce, one example with which I am familiar serves to illustrate the difficulty of such a move. The case involved a successful community college president who had served in her position for ten years. She applied for the presidency of a public four-year college and, although interviewed, was not selected. She next applied for the presidency of a highly respected, four-year private liberal arts college. (In addition to the Ph.D. in higher education, the candidate had a master's degree in history, had traveled abroad for a year, was fluent in French, and was an advocate of liberal education.) Again, she was interviewed but was not selected. In both cases the institutions selected female presidents, thereby ruling out gender as a factor for her rejection. The informal word she received in both instances was that she was not selected because of the "baggage" she brought with her from the community college.

whenever an individual applies for a position and is rejected. Claiming rejection because of one's race, sex, age, or other generic factor permits one to engage in a process of "self-cooling out," whereby one's aspirations are lowered temporarily without destroying one's self-esteem or future ambitions.

To suggest that those presidents who are concerned with the negative images of women that persist in some segments of society are fighting windmills would be to do these women a great disservice and would detract from an understanding of the community college presidency. While it is unlikely that governing boards are engaged in a conspiracy against female candidates for the presidency, the damage to women can be great if the female candidate *perceives* that she is being discriminated against because of her gender during the interview or after assuming office. The foregoing has shown that women do encounter special problems as they move to the top of their profession; whether the problems arise from perception, fact, or ignorance on the part of others, the damage to the woman is likely to be the same.

What do women who aspire to the community college presidency have a right to expect? Certainly they have a right to expect and to demand that double standards be eliminated in the interview process and once they assume office. (One source notes that women who are members of a minority race often face "double discrimination" (Ehrhart and Sandler 1987, p. 8). For example, female applicants should not be asked questions that are not asked of male applicants. A question that may appear innocent to the trustee asking it ("How old are you?" "Are you married?" "Do you have any small children?" "Is your husband willing to move?") can set off a chain reaction in the thinking of the female applicant that may well influence how she conducts herself during the remainder of the interview and could conceivably cause her to perform less well than if she were not faced with answering questions which she views as irrelevant at best and insulting at worst. Moreover, the questions rarely have any bearing on how well the applicant will perform as president. The rule of thumb should be that no questions are asked of a female applicant that are not equally suitable questions for male applicants.

Board members are faced with some special considerations when evaluating women and minority candidates for the presidency. While ensuring that all candidates are treated without prejudice, they should realize that "Women do have some special needs, relating principally to the ways in which they are viewed and treated as members of a class, rather than as separate persons judged on their individual merits" (Shavlik and Touchton 1988, p. 106). Board members, then, have a difficult task in evaluating female and minority candidates' qualifications for a presidency while at the same time ensuring that the decision to employ or not to employ is based on merit rather than sex, race, or ethnic background.

Although women encounter certain difficulties that men do not when seeking the presidency, to assume that being female caused the failure to be selected for a *given* presidency is to greatly oversimplify the presidential selection process. Certainly the nine female presidents who believe that they failed to obtain a presidency because of their sex highlight the need to be more sensitive to the type of questions asked in the interview. On the other hand, they were later selected for presidencies, based in part, one assumes, on the right "fit," a fit that may have been related to their gender.

Trustees are obligated to determine the right fit, or chemistry, for a college at a particular time and location. There are some cases when the right fit requires a white male president and other cases when it requires a female president; in some cases the correct fit may well be a member of a minority race, and in some cases a female member of a minority race may well be the right fit. A black male president, who is in his second presidency of a predominantly white institution and who had been turned down for presidencies prior to obtaining one, offers his analysis of the role fit plays in the presidential selection process. "I do not think being black has been a plus or a negative factor for me. 'Chemistry' is important in presidential selections. In the instances where I was not extended an offer and a white candidate was chosen, my conclusion was that the board's perception of chemistry caused them to turn to another candidate."

A striking example of the role fit plays in presidential selection was illustrated in 1988, when students literally shut down Gallaudet University, the nation's only university for the deaf, because a hearing person was appointed president (DeLoughry, March 16, 1988, pp. A1–A18). As a result of the students' protest, a deaf president was employed, thereby ensuring the proper fit from the perspective of the protesting students. Ironically, perhaps, the president who was let go was female and the one selected was a white male. Selection committees, trustees, and others involved in the presidential selection process must be concerned with the proper fit between the individual and the institution; however, when a president is selected, it is incumbent upon those doing the selecting to be able to demonstrate that the decision to select or not to select an individual was based on considerations other than the gender or race of the applicant, unless indeed gender or race was an important factor in creating the proper fit.

Volumes of literature describe the challenges and frustrations encountered by women moving up the organizational ladder. While the foregoing makes no attempt to explore the literature on women in leadership roles, it its intended to provide a valuable perspective for viewing some of the problems faced by women who aspire to the community college presidency. The comments should help sensitize governing boards and male colleagues to the special problems faced by women in the community college and therefore cause all community college professionals and trustees to view problems more realistically and more compassionately and to eliminate as many sex-related barriers as possible.

AFFIRMATIVE ACTION

Has affirmative action aided women in becoming presidents? Fifty-four percent (nineteen presidents) answered "yes" to the question. Some respondents who said "no" made it clear that affirmative action had changed a number of attitudes, making it easier for women to move to a position in society whereby they could move on to the presidency.

One respondent believes that affirmative action requirements played a significant role in her candidacy. "I was told prior to the interview that I was the best credentialed woman candidate. Affirmative action indicated that it is 'OK' to consider a woman in spite of contrary perceptions that exist. It gave me an opportunity to 'try' and to 'compete.'" Another believes that she was included as *the* female candidate and, after several experiences of being the only woman interviewed, was selected. Affirmative action programs, she believes, "forced college trustees to include women in the pool of applicants and [as a result] some were finally selected." One respondent was quite blunt in her response. "Yes, it [affirmative action] apparently was 'required' by the state chancellor for AA purposes to help him look good." Moreover, she believes that the search committee "needed" a woman and the system "needed" to hire a minority president in order to look good. One respondent notes that, "The governor was committed to *qualified* candidates and especially women and other minority candidates." Another woman president believes that black women often receive "token" interviews to "round out affirmative action records." Other women presidents commented that the board and administration wanted to be sure that they were in line with affirmative action requirements.

Some of the respondents believe the major contribution of affirmative action to be the resulting attitudes in society that go well beyond their own careers, attitudes that nevertheless helped them at various stages in their career. One answer is particularly enlightening in this regard. The female respondent encountered no major difficulties in obtaining the presidency and believes strongly that she was selected because of her accomplishments. Nevertheless, she acknowledges the importance of affirmative action.

In spite of my responses above [regarding no obstacles to the presidency resulting from being a woman] I feel that affirmative action programs did help me to move along in my career. This was particularly true during the earlier period of my career as I was being considered for mid-management

administrative positions and for participation in activities such as the
American Council on Education's academic administrative internship, all of
which gave me the opportunity to build a solid track record of
accomplishments.

One respondent, although stating that affirmative action was not a direct
factor in her obtaining the presidency, believes that it "raised the powers-
that-be consciousness that women are under-represented in executive positions." Another woman president believes that because of affirmative
action the board was seeking a minority candidate but not necessarily a
woman. One president who feels that her credentials got her the initial
interview acknowledges that "it was a brave, but wise, step forward for
this conservative area to select a divorced female." In one case, a president believes that because the board chair was a woman, and an advocate
for women, it was easier for her to obtain the presidency. Donna L. Shavlik, Director of the American Council on Education's Office of Women
in Higher Education, and Judith G. Touchton, Deputy Director, observe
that "Many of these special efforts [leadership programs for women, affirmative action laws and similar undertakings] on behalf of women have
improved the system for everyone. Searches are more open, salaries are
less secretly determined and less discrepant, and people are beginning to
recognize that changing student bodies demand diversity in leadership"
(Shavlik and Touchton 1988, p. 105).
   Certainly the line between being female, a minority, the object of affirmative action programs, and a part of the larger woman's movement is a
blurry one. For example, three respondents stated that being female
helped their candidacy but that affirmative action played no role. One
respondent's answer to the question as to whether being a woman was
an asset in obtaining a presidency illustrates the complexity of trying to
decide where the line between minority, affirmative action, and gender
ends and begins: "I replaced a minority male president. The fact that
women are also under represented among presidents made it easier to
appoint a non-minority candidate to replace a minority." This president
probably profited from the broader aspects of affirmative action; however, had the affirmative action plan for this particular college required
the appointment of a minority president, the female candidate would not
have gotten the presidency.
   Whether being a woman or being under the affirmative action umbrella
is the deciding factor in obtaining the presidency may be a moot point in
the final analysis. Alluding to the role of various social and legislative
forces that have shaped American society during the past two decades,
one source notes:

   All these changes do not necessarily affect the promotion of women leaders
   directly, but they are influential in creating a better climate for the
   acceptance of women as leaders and in increasing the demand for them. . . .

These interventions placed women squarely on the national agenda, not an insignificant part of the advancement experienced by women over the last decade. Women's advocacy groups and organizations . . . and increased visibility of women at national meetings and in the . . . media, all contributed to an increased awareness of women as a vital force in society. (ibid., p. 100)

The major point is that, due in part to affirmative action, society, and therefore governing boards, are aware of the assets women and racial and ethnic minorities bring to the community college presidency. Once members of the governing board and members of the college community recognize the capabilities of presidential candidates other than white males, most presidencies will be filled with the person viewed as being the best qualified to fill a particular vacancy at a particular college at a particular point in time, regardless of gender or race or ethnic background.

MENTORS AND ROLE MODELS

Did the women presidents have mentors? Twenty-seven of the 36 respondents answered "yes" to the question. Eighteen of the 27 respondents stated that they had a male mentor; 3 presidents had a female mentor; 6 presidents had more than one mentor, both male and female; 8 presidents had no mentor; and 1 president did not respond to the question. Mentors ranged from a spouse to a school principal; however, the mentors mentioned most often were community college presidents (15 of the 27 female presidents identified their mentor as a president) deans, and vice presidents.

Role models were also important to women seeking the presidency. Twenty-one of the women presidents stated that they had a role model who influenced their careers. Male dominance in the world of community college administration likely made it difficult for the 18 women who had male mentors to choose a female mentor; however, given a choice, as in the case of choosing a role model, female presidents chose a woman. Of the 13 women presidents who identified a role model other than their mentor (8 identified their mentor as their role model), 10 identified their role model as a woman. Women presidents would seem to have a special obligation to serve as role models and mentors for other women, for as one of the respondents commented, "I was the first woman president in my state—knowing that I could reach the goal was important to me and other women."

NEGATIVE ROLE MODELS

Positive stimulation is one reason individuals advance in their careers, but not the only one. Indeed, a negative situation can often provide the incentive "to break out, to do something." In the survey of female presidents I used the term "negative role model" in an attempt to find out if there were negative experiences that created a desire on the part of the respondents to become a president.

Eighteen of the 35 women presidents (over 51 percent) who responded to the survey stated that they had a negative role model who caused them to want to move up the administrative ladder to become president. Just as presidents often served as role models for the women presidents, they also often served as negative role models for the women presidents. The negative role models varied in their characteristics. Most examples, however, provide insights on leadership and therefore add to the understanding of the community college presidency.

One respondent found that the president she worked under as a dean was "afraid of conflict, hated change and was paralyzed by the prospect of having to make a decision." Another describes her negative role model (again, a president) as a "survivor who did nothing; who put in the minimal time and effort; and who delegated everything." One female president learned some valuable lessons from an "arbitrary, capricious, short-sighted and narrow-minded dean," a dean she never wanted to emulate. And yet another president got her own "inspiration" from a president who "lacked vision, leadership abilities and courage" and who suffered from insecurities. Acting in an autocratic manner, not staying up-to-date in the field, not being bright or creative, and lacking sound judgment were the words one respondent used to describe her negative role model. Two respondents comment on why they sought the presidency. One's comments: "It was not a matter of 'correcting some of the wrongs,' it was rather the realization that I could do the job better—more competently, more efficiently, with less rancor and hostility generated than would be true with someone else." Another respondent stated: "I worked closely with four presidents. I concluded that I could do as well or better than they."

In general, the negative role models possessed characteristics that most people would find distasteful, regardless of gender. In two instances, however, the respondents commented on the role of gender. One commented on a supervisor she had in industry: "He was autocratic and used psychological stress to try to keep me and the few other female employees from progressing in the firm." Another respondent was frustrated by "several women presidents trying to be female versions of their male counter-parts—i.e., suppressing their femininity."

PEER NETWORKS

The ability to identify and become a part of peer networks is often seen as a characteristic of leadership. Peer groups can provide important contacts for those who wish to move up in their profession. Twenty-four of the presidents stated that they were not members of any such group or network. Of the 12 respondents who answered that they were members, 4 replied that the peer group was predominately male, 5 replied that the peer group was predominately female, and 3 replied that the group consisted of males and females equally.

Any number of conclusions could be reached regarding membership in peer groups. One conclusion might be that the majority of the women presidents do not view being a part of a peer network as important to their assuming the presidency, thus implying that there may be too much emphasis placed by some women's groups on calling for an "old girls' network" to serve as a countervailing force to the "old boys' network." One might also conclude that not only is it lonely at the top but also lonely on the way to the top, at least for women moving into the presidency. While 5 respondents identified their peer network as predominately female, the number is not large enough to suggest that women presidents view female peer networks as a major aid in achieving the presidency. Or one might conclude that the provincial nature of the community college itself makes peer group membership difficult and thus not essential to effective leadership. In this respect, those community college presidents identified as leaders by their peers ranked membership in peer groups number sixteen on a list of seventeen skills and abilities leaders should possess (Vaughan 1986, p. 192). All of the above conclusions are tentative, however.

EXTERNAL CONTACTS

Community contacts are often vital to the success of the community college president. Twenty-two of the female presidents identified one or more contacts outside their professional organizations that they believe contributed to their movement into the presidency. Other than the Chamber of Commerce, which was mentioned as important by seven of the respondents, no community contact was mentioned more than once. The contacts—political, religious, the United Way, the YWCA, and individuals, such as a local banker, businessperson, or other members of the local power structure—varied.

PROFESSIONAL ASSOCIATIONS

Is membership in professional organizations important for a woman wanting to become a president? Ten of the respondents failed to identify any professional organization that aided them in their movement into the presidency. The 25 women presidents who identified professional organizations offered a variety of answers. Eight mentioned the American Association of Community and Junior Colleges as being important, and 3 mentioned its affiliate council, the American Association of Women in Community and Junior Colleges; 5 identified the American Association of Higher Education as important; 5 cited the American Council on Education; and 2 mentioned the American Association of University Women. Organizations related to their specific professions (nursing and engineering) were important to 2 respondents. Ten of the respondents referred to professional organizations within their states as significantly aiding them in becoming a president, implying strongly that leadership, like charity, begins at home.

LEADERSHIP PROGRAMS

Fifteen of the women presidents had participated in a program designed to identify and develop leadership skills. The most popular program among the respondents was the American Council on Education's (ACE) National Identification program, in which 7 women presidents had participated; 4 participated in the Leaders for the 80s project; 3 of the 4 also participated in the ACE National Identification program; 2 attended Harvard University's Institute for Educational Management; and 1 each participated in Bryn Mawr's HERS program and the ACE fellows program. A number of other experiences were mentioned, but none with a national reputation for developing future leaders in higher education.

THE ASEXUAL PRESIDENCY

Clark Kerr and Marian Gade (1986) write in *The Many Lives of Academic Presidents* that while women experience special problems in getting appointed to the presidency, once appointed, "Overall, they say they are more readily accepted as time goes on and, 'net,' are not in any better or worse situation than men once they have been appointed. . . ." (p. 118). I used the Kerr and Gade statement as the basis of a question on the survey of women presidents. I asked the female presidents if, once they became president, were they evaluated on how well they perform and not on the fact that they are female presidents; or, stated another way, once someone assumes the presidency, is the assessment of performance asexual? (In the same context, blacks and Hispanics were asked if they viewed the presidency as being "aracial," a term used in conjunction with ethnic as well as racial minorities.)

Twenty-four (66.3 percent) of the respondents stated (some with very minor reservations) that once they assumed the presidency, they found the position to be asexual, an encouraging sign for women aspirants. The eleven other presidents provide some observations on practices relating to gender that continued once they became presidents. One female president responded: "The scrutiny is more intense, and the standards *are* different. I expect this diminishes during one's tenure, for mine is less than one year old." Another offers a similar comment: "Women are scrutinized much more severely and expected to be perfect. Men are allowed errors which women are not allowed." From another: "I feel I may be criticized for something accepted in a man." And yet another: "Expectations of a woman's performances are different from a man's and this leads to assessment against different standards."

At least three women presidents believe that some men and women are uneasy working for a woman. One comments: "I am more aware of being a woman than I ever have been. Part of the problem, though, is that I hired a woman to be the dean of instruction and there are male faculty members and female secretaries who don't like the combination." One respondent states that she has encountered no problems in working with the students or staff. She found, however, that "a few male administrators originally had problems about reporting to a woman, but these have been resolved." She still finds "that male board members have hang-ups about working with a woman." The severest criticism comes from the third president. She states: "Several male staff evidently did not want to work for a female and tried to see to it that I didn't stay. And I'm not staying. Women are criticized more than men for the same actions. Stereotypes are at work. Women are judged by manner rather than actions and decisions."

Some female presidents alluded to both subtle and not-so-subtle forms of sexism. From one: "I feel that there is still an underlying attitude that has a sexual basis and actions are often judged by comparison with those a man might make." From another: "The issue is never put to rest. I have been under constant attack (overt and covert) by men since I assumed the presidency." The following statement from one of the respondents illustrates a subtle form of sexism that still exists in some situations: "Faculty perceive my administration as being female dominated because of the top administration; there are now five women and 12 men. A female president at another college told me that her administration is perceived as female even though she has not changed the mix of females to males since assuming the presidency." Is the community college presidency asexual? Not totally. Should it be? Probably not, since the female president can bring a dimension to the position that is often missing in male presidents.

One woman president detects no discrimination from within the institution; however, she believes that "external to the institution women encounter the same subtle effects of sexism." Another respondent notes: "As far as working with my staff, I don't think being a woman is much of an issue. A major obstacle to overcome is becoming part of the community's 'power base.' For instance, clubs like Rotary exclude women.[3] I

[3]Eight-six percent of all community college presidents reported that they belong to a service club; 65 percent of all community college presidents reported that they belong to the Rotary Club, by far the most popular service club in terms of the community college presidency (Vaughan 1986, p. 24). Women's perception of the Rotary membership as being important to the presidency may be exaggerated; however, women's views of the Rotary as an "all-male club" are correct in most instances, although recent legal decisions have caused some Rotary clubs to offer membership to women.

therefore need to work closely with organizations such as United Way and the Chamber of Commerce to build relationships." Another woman president notes that she "sometimes gets discouraged about being the token woman in statewide CEO activities, committees, etc." She also notes that she is "excluded from community 'power' clubs that are for men only." Another expresses similar feelings: "I've had to find ways to become acquainted with male community members other than Rotary. The local press insisted on addressing me as 'Mrs.' and not Dr. They have since changed their policy because the press reps respect me. The board wanted a complete new image in our district and I certainly did that—from my appearance to the management of our college."

OCCUPYING THE OFFICE

Are there any advantages to being a female president? Or, in the context of the above discussion, are there advantages that accrue to female presidents because the position is not totally asexual? Fourteen of the 35 women presidents responding to the survey feel that they enjoy certain advantages in the presidency because they are women. (Three of the 11 who said that the presidency is not asexual believe that there are advantages that accrue from being a female president.) One president believes because she is a woman she is "more interested in solving problems than winning my particular point." Another believes that as a woman she is "not perceived as a threat to most powerful males." Another female president feels that she can be firm without being viewed as threatening. Another states: "In interpersonal relations, I do not have to be as authoritarian, especially with male colleagues."

Advantages and disadvantages of being a woman seeking and occupying the community college presidency, like truth and beauty, are often in the eyes of the beholder. For example, some respondents believe that "female characteristics" that are viewed as disadvantages by some women are viewed as advantages by others. (The truth is that whether "female characteristics" are advantages or disadvantages depends upon the situation and the individual.) From one: "I can show my emotions (joy, disappointment, etc.) more spontaneously and thereby be able to relate more personally with faculty and administrative colleagues as well as with students. I often let my motherly instincts guide me in dealing with them." In a similar vein: "As a woman and a mother I have had different cultural experiences from most men. I believe it has made me more patient, understanding and able to endure difficult situations than if I had been raised as most men are." Another comment: "Women are more used to listening to family spats and possibly can be fairer in judging situations." Another believes that faculty are "less confrontational" because she is a woman president. One believes: "I feel that I am more approachable and that people often confide more readily in me because I am a woman." Similarly, "Men tend to confide in me more because I am female and exhibit their emotions more openly."

One female president likes the balance she is able to bring to the presidency, in part because of her gender. "I often find myself combining my skills as an administrator and my knack as a social hostess in working with my many constituencies within the university [the community colleges in her state are a part of the university system] as well as in the community. I can make a person feel at ease and then deal with the business at hand. Very simply put, enjoying being a woman is the best way to enjoy my life as an administrator." From another: "Because the majority of people who report to me are male, I feel there is less posturing and we have more open relationships than would be the case with people of the same sex." Another notes that being a woman president makes her somewhat unique; therefore, she receives a "great deal of positive press and is included in many groups" because she is a female president. Similarly another notes, "I'm a curiosity in the community. People seem to want to know what I look like, what I sound like, etc." From another respondent: "On occasion, I feel I am treated as an 'oddity' by some members of the community, and I choose to view this positively." And, finally, one of the female presidents makes a comment that will win the hearts and support of hundreds of male presidents from across the nation. Is there an advantage to being a woman president? "Yes. I don't have to join the Rotary Club!" was her reply. However, even this is changing. On the other hand, some things never change. One respondent added the following postscript to her survey. "I am currently five months' pregnant and the reaction has been great!"

Chapter

6

THE MINORITY PRESIDENTS

We hold these truths to be self-evident, that all men are created
equal. . . .
—The Declaration of Independence July 4, 1776

We must never forget that all Americans have the right to pursue the
American Dream; we must never forget that the community college
represents the only hope millions of Americans have of achieving that
Dream.
—George B. Vaughan

As suggested in the introduction to Chapters 5 and 6, minority presidents
are important to the current and future status of the community college
in the United States. The importance of minority presidents, especially
blacks and Hispanics, will increase as the number of minority students
grow. Minority presidents, perhaps even more than female presidents,
must be sensitive to the need to serve as role models for future leaders
of their own race and ethnic group. They must also realize that the community college's mission to serve all segments of society cannot be
achieved without the leadership of minorities.

BLACKS

The survey was sent to 48 black presidents; 26 returned it, for a response
rate of slightly over 54 percent. The responses came from 17 states, with
the largest number responding from California (5 presidents representing

19 percent of the total). Two responses were received from 5 states, with 1 response each from the remaining 11 states.

Pathway to the Presidency

Just as society clings to stereotypical images of women, blacks also suffer from stereotyping. As a result, the images some members of society have of blacks caused some black presidents difficulties on their pathway to the presidency.

Based upon a number of responses, the major stereotyping that occurs with black community college presidents is that some governing boards view them as being suited to lead urban, predominantly black institutions but not suburban, predominantly white ones. For example, one black president, although selected for the presidency of an institution where the majority of the students are white, was faced with the perception that the institution was "not ready" for a black president. Another respondent observes that

> The difficulty most Blacks face is that one can probably become president of an institution that has been traditionally perceived as serving a minority, Black population. However, it is almost impossible to be considered seriously for the presidency of a majority college even though one may possess impressive credentials and experience. While progress has been made in terms of institutional racism, there are still major impediments to Black presidents achieving full equality. Thus, the struggle continues.

Similarly, from another respondent: "I was channeled into a stereotyped urban institution serving minorities. There is no real access to a range of institutions for the black president." From another: "Having reached the level of dean, the only institutions interested in employing me [as president] were predominantly black institutions." And another found a major obstacle to be the difficulty of "finding the right 'fit' for a black person." One president believes that stereotypes associated with blacks are definitely handicaps for those who aspire to the presidency. A result is the "belief that a Black professional should be in an urban environment, in an inner-city college rather than a suburban one," observes one black president.

While the many issues associated with being black in the United States are well beyond this discussion, one response from a black president serves to remind those persons interested in the community college presidency of both the inherent promise of the American dream and the agony of pursuing it as a black in America. His response: "The major obstacle for me was the fact that I was born of extremely poor black and virtually uneducated parents in a hostile society."

The open access community college is committed to decreasing poverty, illiteracy, and hostility in our society. If the community college is successful, especially in serving members of the lower socioeconomic groups, future black presidents may not have to overcome some of the difficulties current black presidents had to overcome on their pathway to the presidency.

The Interview. Do governing boards ask questions relating to one's race? In the case of black presidents, the answer is "not often." Yet some boards do ask questions of blacks that likely would not be asked of whites. For example, a board inquired of one successful presidential candidate: "Are you really serious? This is a big school and it's mostly white." The same individual felt that he had been turned down for a previous presidency because the selection committee simply "could not see" a black being accepted at the college or being able to do the job if selected. During an interview another president was asked by a faculty member and by the search committee if he would be able to adjust to an environment that had no minority professionals and very few minority students.

A female black president, while not asked any questions relating to sex or race during the interview for her current position, feels that in past interviews she was "definitely" turned down because of race. She recalls: "A group of faculty members made it clear to the search committee that a black candidate would be unacceptable." Their reasoning was that "since it was a predominantly white suburban college, the president should reflect the community." One successful candidate was asked his definition of affirmative action. His response: "If I am not *the* best candidate, pick someone else!" Nevertheless, the respondent's answer on another question serves to remind us that stereotypes do indeed die hard. The board consultant, who obviously had not done his "homework," asked the same individual how he would provide leadership as a black person in a predominantly white institution, implying that by being black he might have problems that a white president would not have. What the consultant did not know was that the applicant was currently the president of a predominantly white institution and had been in the position for a number of years.

Although the number of questions related to race asked during the interviews was few, can blacks assume that race is not an issue in presidential selections? Probably not. The above questions demonstrate that even today, in some instances, questions relating to race are asked. In addition, most segments of society have become very sensitive to the "race issue" and avoid questions that can be interpreted as racist. The fact may be that if race is to be an issue in presidential selection, the issue has clearly been settled during the screening process, at least from the perspective of the governing board. As a result, blacks are interviewed for the presidencies of predominantly black institutions, thereby eliminating any questions relating to race that might have been asked under other circumstances.

The issue of race raises the question of how closely the president of a community college should mirror the larger community. Certainly the "fit" between community and president should be right; however, if the president mirrors the values of the community too closely, objectivity might be lost and the institution itself may be devoted solely to preserving the status quo rather than bringing about change. While one can argue that a purpose of an institution of higher education is to preserve established values, one can also argue that a purpose is to bring about change. The ideal president should maintain the objectivity to decide what to preserve and what to change, a situation that may not exist if the president's values match those of the community too closely.

As is true with most presidential selections, blacks rarely were asked about the role of the spouse. Only two presidents, one male and one female, were asked any questions relating to the role of the spouse; neither question was related to the role of the spouse as a member of the presidential team. One was asked if his wife supported him in his decision to apply for the position. In the other instance, some students asked the candidate questions regarding the spouse's role because of, as she notes, "the inter-racial nature of my marriage."

Assets and Liabilities

What are the assets and liabilities associated with being a black candidate for the presidency? Are the lines clear enough to determine whether being black is an advantage or disadvantage? Are blacks rejected because of their race? Or are blacks included in the pool of applicants because of their race? These are some of the questions discussed in relationship to women; the answers to these questions given by blacks also help one to understand the community college presidency and the presidential selection process.

Was being a black applicant a factor in the presidential selection process? Twelve presidents responded that being black was neither an asset nor a liability; 10 saw being black as an asset; and 4 saw being black as a liability.

Perceived Liabilities. One black president believes that he was passed over for promotions earlier in his career because of his race. Another believes that in some instances his application was thrown out because of "identifiable Black affiliations" on his résumé. Another feels that the opportunities to gain experience are more limited for blacks than for whites and that he was faced with breaking into the "good-old-boy" network. Similarly, another believes that a major obstacle to blacks moving into the presidency is the failure of whites to accept black leadership.

One black president believes that being black was a liability because "it was assumed that I was a 'token' interviewee for affirmative action purposes; thus, I had to work harder to ensure that I was taken seriously as a *bona fide* candidate." Another believes that being black is a liability, "although it is not spoken." One believes that those doing the interviewing are concerned about "acceptance on and off campus for Black appointees and [acceptance] in 'social situations' about which they fantasize."

Perceived Assets. Ten of the black presidents perceived their race as an asset in obtaining the presidency. Ironically, many of the perceived advantages of being black in a specific case are often not transferrable into the larger realm of the community college presidency, or at least this appears to be the case based upon what the black presidents said regarding obstacles to the position and the type of institution for which they were considered a good "fit."

A quote from a president illustrates the "Catch-22" situation facing blacks as they move into the presidential ranks. "I felt that being black was an asset in the situation where the student population was mostly black. But in a situation where blacks were a small minority, people seemed concerned about my ability to adjust." Another saw being black as an asset because "the college is 70% black in terms of student population. The city in which the college is located is over 70% black in population." One president notes that an "institution named after an identified 'Black Militant' would obviously need a person of my color and persuasion. Race seemed to be a condition to qualify for consideration. . . ." One person was very "up front" in his response, as was the governing board in stating its requirements. "Being black was an asset because only a black person was going to be hired. This was stated clearly in the 'Position Announcement.' " From another president: "Yes, being black was an asset. The school has a 96% black enrollment. The community is black and politically active. The board has an affirmative action plan and is sensitive to community interests." Similarly, "The college of which I am president is predominantly black and is located in a predominantly black community. Having a president who could also function as a role model for the college and the community was though to be critical." One president notes that being black was an asset because in the city in which the college is located the black population is over 55 percent of the total population and growing; moreover, the "governor promised the black community that the next president at the institution would be black." And from another: "The fact that I was Black was an asset because those institutions that I interviewed with had large minority student bodies, and they were seeking a candidate that was both sensitive to and experienced in dealing with such populations." Finally from another, "Being Black was an asset because it provided a unique perspective for the ——— Community College System as well as for the college. Likewise, students, faculty and staff would have an increased opportunity to learn about people from diverse backgrounds.''

One president sheds light on the presidency in relationship to the larger society.

> It is my belief that we still live in a society where standards of performance are applied differently to various ethnic groups and individuals within those groups. Performance within a multi-ethnic society has requirements which differ from group to group. A black president is ''expected'' to champion affirmative action causes, as an example. To generalize, there is a set of beliefs and behaviors which are expected of a black president which may or may not be expected of others. Such expectations require a special awareness and ability to provide presidential leadership in a very balanced and sensitive manner.

It appears that blacks aspiring to the majority of the community college presidencies may well face frustrations resulting in part from their race because, although race appears to be an asset in some situations, it is a limiting factor unless the black candidate is interested in a particular type of institution. On the other hand, governing boards of all community colleges should realize that if a black president is an effective leader of an inner-city, predominantly black institution (certainly among the most difficult leadership positions in all of higher education), then he or she should succeed equally as well in a suburban institution, regardless of its racial composition.

With the above in mind, anyone interested in the community college presidency should remember that fit is important in the selection of a president. One of the black presidents alludes to fit, or chemistry. His response: ''This is my second presidency in a predominantly white setting; therefore, I do not think that being black has been a plus or negative factor. 'Chemistry' is important in presidential selections. In the instances where I was not extended an offer and a white candidate was, my conclusion is that the board's perception of chemistry caused them to turn to another candidate.'' Certainly a governing board has every right to know if a black presidential applicant who has worked in institutions with a majority of black students and residents feels that he or she perceives any difficulty in being the president of a predominantly white institution in a white suburb. A danger is that in the case of black presidents, fit might be interpreted to mean that the fit is right only if the student population and population in general are predominantly black, an interpretation that promotes stereotyping, and one that penalizes blacks and ultimately penalizes the community college, for ''democracy's college'' can know no color lines in selecting its top leaders if it is ever to reach its full potential as an institution of higher education devoted to serving all Americans.

Affirmative Action

Has affirmative action aided blacks in becoming presidents? Fourteen (over 53 percent) of the 26 respondents answered "yes" to the question. One respondent notes that the "so called movement of the '60s transformed the institution" of which he is president, making it imperative that the president be black. Another notes that "the VP position was established for a black person to learn about the presidency. When the vacancy arose, I was appointed president." In another instance, the "committee actively sought a diverse pool of applicants" which included blacks. From another: "Yes, a strong affirmative action plan/policy keeps this issue at the forefront. However, I think this board would have hired a competent person of color without a policy or plan." Another: "Yes, the board and the chancellor are convinced that affirmative action and *equal access* are facts of life." Another: "Yes, efforts to include qualified blacks and other minorities and women in the applicant pool and to consider them fairly was important." Another: "My institution committed itself to having a fair and representative number of minorities in all areas. I happened to be available and qualified." One successful candidate found it useful being "registered with the affirmative action vita bank" and believes that "AA gave me an opportunity for an interview but nothing beyond that." Finally, one black president noted that being black was not helpful in obtaining the interview, but nevertheless acknowledges the impact of affirmative action on the larger society. His response: "The social and political environment that supported affirmative action programs made my becoming a college president feasible."

While over 50 percent of the blacks state that affirmative action played no role in their obtaining the presidency, the civil rights movement of the 1960s that resulted in part in affirmative action laws certainly created an awareness of the unacceptable state of affairs as far as equal opportunity for blacks and women was concerned. The success of affirmative action is still being debated. Indeed, Reginald Wilson, Director, and Sarah Meléndez, Associate Director of the American Council on Education's Office of Minority Concerns, believe that

> When pressed by federal government and the courts to increase diversity, white institutions were more comfortable with increasing opportunities for white women who were perceived as being more compatible with the norms and values of the academy. As a further irony, the initial civil rights laws promulgated originally to assist minorities, ended by benefitting majority women more than the minorities who were the initial target group. (Wilson and Meléndez 1988, p. 122)

Nevertheless, in the case of black presidents, affirmative action has made governing boards more sensitive to the need to consider blacks as potential presidents.

On the other hand, the role of affirmative action may be even more complicated for blacks than for women, for there are no public "women's community colleges" in the sense that a woman would be appointed president—would be the right fit—because of the number of women in the student body or in the community. Yet as several black presidents point out, some governing boards appoint black presidents for colleges with a majority of blacks in the student body, thereby satisfying affirmative action goals without truly integrating the presidency. That is, being black could help one to obtain the presidency of a predominantly black institution in much the same way as being a woman and Catholic could help one obtain the presidency of a Catholic women's college. In either case, affirmative action would likely not play a direct role.

Indeed, in those cases where a black candidate is appointed to the presidency of a predominantly black community college, affirmative action may be deemed a failure, for rather than integrating the presidency and offering true equal opportunity, affirmative action preserves the status quo, a status quo that has its roots deep in the history of American higher education, a history that has often failed to utilize the talents of minorities to the fullest. In the final analysis, the major contribution of affirmative action as far as the community college presidency is concerned may be that, as one respondent noted above, "it keeps this issue at the forefront" and therefore helps ensure that blacks are among the applicants and have the opportunity to be judged on their qualifications and abilities and not on preconceived notions about blacks.

Mentors and Role Models

Did black presidents have mentors? Ten of the 26 respondents stated that they had a mentor; 6 of the 10 had community college presidents as their mentors; 2 had vice presidents and 2 had professors. Two of the 10 identified their mentor as being black; 3 stated that they had both white and black mentors.

An overwhelming majority (21 out of 26, or over 86 percent) of the black presidents had a role model who influenced their career. While 6 of the role models were also mentors, 15 of the black presidents had role models other than their mentor. Twelve presidents had black role models, ranging from one's father and another's mother to an uncle to a high school teacher to college presidents and professors. As with women, blacks would seem to have a special obligation to serve as role models and mentors to other blacks until that time when blacks are represented at the presidential level in an equitable fashion. A touching statement from one of the respondents says so much about the need for mentors and role models in society in general and specifically in the community college. His comment: "I always wanted a mentor. Unfortunately, there were too few available. I think I am now serving as a parttime mentor to four younger colleagues.'' Presidents of all races and both sexes can learn from this president.

Negative Role Models

Eight of the black presidents responding to the survey stated that they had ''negative role models.'' Six of the eight negative role models were community college presidents. One was ''arbitrary and capricious toward personnel and insensitive toward students.'' Another was an ''autocratic demagogue of questionable integrity who was unable to get cohesive support and to move the college to quick and decisive gains.'' ''A college president with poor management and communications skills, autocratic in style, and lacking in sensitivity in human relations'' was how another black president described his negative role model. Other presidents who had negative influences on future black presidents lacked vision, were not creative, and had limited abilities as leaders. Yet another president who served as a negative role model ''demonstrated a lack of aggressive leadership during a time when direct presidential action was needed and called for during the late 1960s and early 1970s.'' One black president describes the influence of his negative role model as follows: ''I wanted to be a president anyway, and I tried to learn from a negative experience.''

Peer Networks

Of the 26 black presidents responding to the survey, 5 stated that they were members of a peer network. Of the 5, only one stated that the peer network consisted primarily of blacks. One respondent stated that he did not belong to a peer group consisting primarily of blacks because ''Prior to my forming the 'Black Presidents' Round Table' none existed.'' None of the respondents listed the National Council of Black American Affairs as providing them with a peer network, thus implying that the council, while perhaps being an important professional association for blacks (3 presidents listed it as a professional organization that aided them in becoming a president), does not appear to provide the close associations normally associated with a peer network.

How important is a peer network? One source believes that ''minorities are . . . excluded from significant administrative positions by virtue of their exclusion from the 'old boy network,' which appears to be alive and well. While many white women have been able to penetrate these ranks in recent years, minority professionals generally have not. When majority leaders are asked to recommend individuals for positions, they naturally look to those in their network'' (Wilson and Melendez 1988, p. 128).

External Contacts

Eighteen of the 26 black presidents responding to the survey stated that external contacts were important in their movement into the presidency. Eight of the 18 identified at least one black group or organization as being influential. Most important among the black groups and organizations were black churches and the National Association for the Advancement of Colored People, each of which was listed by 4 presidents. Other organizations ranged from the "black underground" to the YMCA to the Urban League to state and local political groups. Based upon the responses, it does not appear that blacks are any more likely to align themselves with predominantly black organizations than with any other group. Indeed, one black president—the same one who found that once he wanted to move into the presidency that the only institutions interested in employing him were predominantly blacks ones—believes that his most important nonprofessional contacts external to the campus came from attending predominantly white schools and interacting with whites since childhood. Only one black president stated that the Chamber of Commerce was an important external. This is somewhat surprising considering that serving on the chamber's board of directors is an important civic activity for community college presidents (Vaughan 1986, p. 25) and considering the community college's much vaunted business-industry partnership.

Professional Associations

Ten of the black presidents listed one or more professional associations that aided them in becoming a president. The organizations varied: a regional accrediting agency; American Association of Higher Education; Phi Delta Kappa; American Association of University Professors; National Association of College and University Business Officers; American Association of Community and Junior Colleges, listed by three presidents; Council on Black American Affairs, listed by three presidents; and Black Presidents' Round Table, listed by two presidents. No state organizations were listed by black presidents as aiding them in their movement into the presidency.

Leadership Programs

Eleven of the black presidents stated that they had participated in a program to develop leaders in higher education prior to becoming a president. Four of the 11 presidents had participated in Harvard's Institute for Educational Management; 2 listed the community college leadership program at the University of Texas, Austin; and the 5 others listed various programs, including those sponsored by the Danforth Foundation, the Carnegie Foundation, and the Rockefeller Foundation. None of the respondents listed the McKnight Black Doctoral Fellowship Program in

Florida, a program that seems to hold potential for blacks interested in becoming presidents (Wilson and Melendez 1988, p. 131), and none of the presidents listed the American Council on Education's Fellows Program, a somewhat surprising finding since of the 812 fellows who have gone through the program, 19 percent were minorities and from 1981 to 1986, 26 percent of the fellows were minorities (Wilson and Melendez 1988, p. 129).

The "Aracial" Presidency?

Using Kerr and Gade's observations regarding the academic presidency as being asexual, I asked the black presidents if they felt that the presidency was "aracial." Eighteen (over 69 percent of the respondents) indicated that they do not consider the presidency to be aracial. Seven answered "yes," the presidency is "aracial"; and 1 black woman president responded that "It happens that I am a woman and black women still experience difficulties as women," implying that she encounters problems as a result of being a female president as well as from being black.

The comments on the racial aspects of the presidency provide enlightening observations on the position. A number of black presidents believe that a "double standard" exists by which the performance of black presidents is judged. The following quotes, all from different presidents, express these sentiments: "There are still two standards that the larger society uses to evaluate minority presidents. Institutional racism continues to influence one's assessment of the performance of a minority president. Therefore, in order to be considered average, I have to be better than average." "Blacks have to be even better. There is always the question of does a black have the ability. However, I'm quite accustomed to that question and use that energy-producing assertion to be better at my profession." "The presidency is not totally 'aracial' because there are those who tend to view black institutions and their leaders as somehow being less competent unless they prove otherwise. Black leaders, therefore, must perform in such a way as to dispel or refute erroneous assumptions about their competency, whereas white leaders do not." "I have been referred to as 'one of the best black presidents' and not just one of the best presidents." "If the assessment is made by whites it will almost always be made in comparison to other blacks. I have had the statement made—unwittingly—that 'you are the best black president in the state,' followed by an apology." "It is almost impossible to describe. My board is superb and totally color blind; however faculty frequently place demands on a black president in terms of standards seldom demanded of my white predecessors." "Being black is always different. Blacks have always wanted to be evaluated on performance and not on the fact that one is black. Racism in our society has made that an almost impossible possibility." "Often I feel that a black president has to be much more concerned about issues of quality and academic and fiscal respectability. It's more difficult (but not impossible) to penetrate certain power and social circles. In addition to regular responsibilities, there are many, many outside activities which draw on your time simply because you are black." "Because there are so few black presidents it becomes incumbent on the few to fill a disproportionate number of local and national roles. Like the presidency, the fact of our blackness requires exceptional performance on all fronts. These additional responsibilities do not excuse us from our presidencies or our community leadership responsibilities as role models." " 'Aracial,' absolutely not! Our society is becoming increasingly racist again. Thus people's reactions to CEO's are being increasingly affected by race. This creates awkward situations for a Black CEO since one must sort reactions to the issue from reactions to the man's race. Educators have been sharply isolated from one another and separated by race. This makes communication difficult across racial lines among people who should be peers. I find my white peers uncomfortable with me and ill at ease. It's their problem. I have had to relate and work with whites and others all my life. Perhaps there is a dimension missing in *their* education." Certainly these presidents leave little doubt that they perceive that blacks are judged by stricter standards than are white presidents.

Other comments from black presidents who reject the presidency as being aracial provide valuable insights into the presidency. A black woman responded to the question on the aracial nature of the presidency as follows: "A woman president is judged-evaluated on how well she performs as a president and on how well she performs as a president who is female. The same holds true for a Black president, and if the Black president happens to also be a woman, then she is evaluated on three bases." Others allude to the larger society's impact on blacks: "I believe a strong effort is made to be 'aracial,' but because of the role race has played in American society since the 17th century, it is very difficult to view a black person in isolation of race." "My colleagues are always aware that I am black. All of the social and political cultures of the U.S. are keenly aware of the existence of black folk. To include my blackness in a judgment of my performance is inevitable." "While I think the primary focus becomes one of competence, such concerns as 'style' and 'human relations' based on race remain on the minds of some people." "Our society is not capable of neutral assessments with regard to race and gender." "I am convinced that the Black president is in a 'Catch-22' position. If he/she fails, the stereotype of incompetence is reinforced. If he/she succeeds, he/she becomes a threat to others' egos and expectations."

Two black presidents refer to the "prejudgment" that takes place. From one: "The visual impact, the manners I use, my appearance, my personal acumen are judged before my ability." From another: "A Black

CEO is viewed as precisely that. Reactions to him are dualistic, as a CEO *and* as a Black. Tough role!''

One female black president who views being black as an advantage in her current position believes that the importance of one's race in relationship to the presidency diminishes over time. ''After having been a president for two years, I am passing into another phase of evaluation. The emphasis is less on the Black and more on the president, and yet I am often referred to as a Black president by external groups or as a woman president. Changes occur very slowly.'' She continues: ''My being Black has not interfered with such factors as decision-making, power, communications, etc. I have had to pass through academic rituals, jump the hurdles, and prove my worth as any president irrespective of race.''

One black president's response to the question has implications well beyond the question, for the latter part of his answer might well describe the situation of most presidents, regardless of sex or race. His response: ''The official assessors (the board, etc.) are 'aracial.' The unofficial raters (the community members) by and large are 'racial' for several years. *After several years of super performance one can be accepted as long as everything goes well''* [italics added]. Such, one can safely say, is the nature of the position.

Occupying the Office

Are there advantages to being a black president? Twelve of the respondents see certain advantages to being black. The most often mentioned advantage to being black is in establishing relationships with the black community. The following quotes, each from a different president, illustrate these perceived advantages: ''It is easier to move within or throughout the community (55% black) and the public school system (75% black).'' ''At times, dealing with the Black community or other minority groups is somewhat easier because of the ability to relate or [because of] common backgrounds. This is true for me but not necessarily true for all Blacks.'' ''Yes, there is easier accessibility to black community organizations and to possible benefactors who have a particular interest in minority educational and economic development.'' ''Yes, the constituency—faculty, students, neighborhood, elected officials—are predominantly black.'' ''A black president is perceived as being able to deal with issues relative to minority students without difficulty.'' ''Yes, relationship building in the minority community.'' ''I understand the population of the city (70 percent black) in which the college is located. I understand and support the aspirations of the student body (70 percent black).'' ''I honestly feel that I could not do the kind of job that I am doing at this point in time in this community if I were other than black.'' ''This college was created out of the tumult of the civil rights movement of the '60s. The mandate, goal, or mission for this college was to service a minority community *in that community*. Being black will not hurt *anyone* who serves as president of this institution." One black woman president believes that "My work with ethnic communities has been greatly enhanced because I have an entree to them which would not have been possible for a white president. I am in greater demand as a Black president to serve on statewide committees and local boards because of the different perspective I have as a Black person. I have consulted with state universities in the area of Black student recruitment and retention."

Two presidents who see being black as an asset qualified their answers. From one: "This is a qualified *yes*. The community residents and the student body are primarily Black; however, expectations among them often weigh more heavily than the power invested in the college presidency in this system." From the other one: "Yes, but only in the black community and only sometimes."

Respondents perceive other advantages to being a black president. One believes that certain expectations are not made of him because he is black. Also, he notes that "criticism is often made without foundation and not to you directly." One sees a somewhat perverse advantage in being a black president. She notes: "There are no assumptions that there will be automatic support or that anything will be easy." Another answer is equally as biting: "Yes, one is always needed to 'sit by the door,' so I get to sit by the door a lot."

As the community college and its presidents endeavor to serve all Americans, black presidents must be brought into the mainstream of the presidency and placed in positions to open doors rather than sit by them. Or, as one source notes in reference to all minorities: "Minorities cannot just be the foot soldiers in this country's continued struggle for leadership . . .; they must be among the high command as well, which decides the direction of leadership" (Wilson and Melendez 1988, p. 135). Nevertheless, the perceived advantages of being black tend to present black presidents and governing boards with something of a dilemma: in certain colleges, being black can be a decided advantage for the president because the fit is right. On the other hand, if blacks are especially adept at serving as presidents of primarily black institutions and their effectiveness is not viewed in the larger realm of national community college leadership, their very effectiveness may close the doors of opportunity to them should they wish to serve predominantly white institutions, thereby depriving the nation's two-year colleges and the nation itself of much needed leadership.

While one should not assume that blacks prefer predominantly white institutions over predominantly black ones, blacks as well as others should be able to compete on an equal basis for *any* presidency they desire, regardless of the makeup of the student body and the community. Indeed, the ability of the president to relate to minorities and to serve as a role model for all students may be just as important—or even more so—in a predominantly white institution with few minorities, minorities who may need understanding, attention, and inspiration more than members of a minority race at an institution where the majority of the students are members of a minority race. Moreover, the black president at a predominantly white institution can help white students to understand and appreciate the contributions of minorities. One black scholar who teaches at a predominantly white university speaks to the importance of having black leaders on predominantly white campuses:

> We have an obligation and responsibility to the black students at our institutions to help them get through, and to show our white students that scholarly achievement knows no color. But, in addition, we have hope that our white colleagues will eventually put aside their stereotypes, prejudice, and misconceptions, and that together we can make our institutions and our society better places for all of us. (Harvey 1987, p. 49)

HISPANICS

The survey was sent to 18 Hispanic presidents; 10 returned it, for a response rate of 55.5 percent. The responses came from 6 states, with the largest number responding from California (4 presidents representing 40 percent of the total). Two responses were received from New Jersey and 1 each from Arizona, Florida, New Mexico, and Texas.

Pathway to the Presidency

Hispanic presidents encountered some of the same obstacles in their move to the presidency as did women and blacks, but not to the same degree. One Hispanic president believes that he and a Hispanic colleague had to prove themselves more than did majority presidents. He observes: "My first presidency was in New Jersey, and I was appointed in an 'acting capacity' for six months. A second Hispanic, also in New Jersey, was appointed in an acting capacity for a year. No Caucasian went through that process." Another found an "unwillingness [on the part of administrators] to accept a Hispanic as their superior." Another felt that there was a perceived lack of confidence on the part of some that a minority president could be competent and a belief that a minority person could work effectively only with minorities. From another: "A major obstacle was the perception that a Hispanic may not have the fortitude to be a college president." He also noted that he lacked a network of peers among Hispanic presidents and that subtle elements of discrimination remain at work in today's society. One Hispanic president provides an insightful comment on the lack of a peer network to serve Hispanics who aspire to the presidency: "We are at the point in California where we are finally establishing an effective Hispanic network. In the future this may assist other Hispanic administrators to aspire to the presidency. Too many young Hispanics feel that this position is beyond their grasp because of the small number of Hispanics who are currently presidents.'' Another Hispanic president believes that the ''more conservative communities are not ready for a minority president.'' Another Hispanic president (from California) listed English not being his native language as a barrier to his movement into the presidency.

Hispanic community college presidents have not been the focus of national attention as have women and black presidents. Ironically, the lack of attention on Hispanics may mean that many of them do not aspire to higher level positions to the same degree that women and blacks do, for many young Hispanic administrators may well see the presidency ''beyond their grasp.'' Stated another way, Hispanics may not have internalized the belief that ''you too can make it'' to the same degree that blacks and women have been told that they too can ''make it.'' If a position is seen as beyond's one grasp, it is unlikely that one will aspire to it. If the American community college is to achieve its potential as an institution devoted to serving all Americans, Hispanics must be encouraged to seek the presidency, for without Hispanic leadership many of the community college's future students will be without role models and the movement as a whole will suffer for lack of an important perspective at the top leadership level.

The Interview. Were Hispanic presidents asked questions relating to their ethnic identity when they were interviewed for the presidency? Not often. One trustee asked a candidate if he would be able to work with a diverse population. Another was asked the extent to which he was involved in promoting bilingual education and if there were benefits to such a practice. Another respondent, in an unsuccessful attempt at obtaining a presidency, was asked ''why so many Hispanics were on welfare.'' And a faculty member asked him during the interview ''why there were so many revolutions all the time in Latin America.'' None of the ten respondents were asked any questions relating to the role of the spouse in relationship to the presidency.

Can Hispanics assume that ethnicity is not an issue in presidential selections? As with blacks, if one's ethnic background is an issue it has probably been dealt with from the board's perspective prior to beginning the actual selection process. On the other hand, based on the ten responses, it does not appear that Hispanics face stereotyping to the degree that blacks and women do. Moreover, although the states where the Hispanic presidents are located have large Hispanic populations, the responding Hispanic presidents gave no indication that they were limited to colleges with large Hispanic populations, a sharp contrast to the perceptions of black presidents.

Assets and Liabilities

What are the assets and liabilities associated with being a Hispanic candidate for the presidency? Was being Hispanic even a factor in the presidential selection process?

Perceived Liabilities. The perceived liabilities associated with being Hispanic and seeking a community college presidency appear minor. Why? The answers are complex. One answer might be that the small number of Hispanic presidents has not had enough of an impact nationally to generate any great amount of discussion. Another might be that the large Hispanic populations are limited to a relatively small number of states. And yet another answer might lie in the diversity of the geographic origins of Hispanic Americans, a diversity that does not exist with black presidents or with most women presidents.

Perceived Assets. The perceived assets of being a Hispanic and seeking the presidency were minor, according to those responding to the survey. One president acknowledged that his race was an "added plus" but noted that his "track record as a dean was the most important factor." Another president noted that the composition of the student body was largely Hispanic and that his being Hispanic was a "political necessity." Two presidents were not certain as to whether being Hispanic was an asset or a liability. From one: "I'm not certain. It's possible, however, that being Hispanic played a part simply because I am in a community where the Hispanic influence is very strong, economically and politically." From the other: "I don't know. I'd like to think that I was selected because I was the best man for the job. The total Hispanic population in this county is less than 10%—there was obviously no community pressure for my selection." One president responded wryly to the question regarding being Hispanic as an asset. His response: "In Seattle?"

One Hispanic president believes that his race helped him to obtain his first presidency but not his current one. (If correct, this president's views would support the belief that it is much easier to move from one presidency to another than to move from some other position to the presidency.) Another president comments: "Yes, I believe being Hispanic helped; however, my professional experiences, my academic credentials, and, perhaps, sense of presence among key community and state educators helped in this case. I was a good candidate who happened to be Hispanic!" Another believes that "being Hispanic was a hurdle, in New Jersey, that is. I don't believe it made any difference in California. The search committee and board knew me by reputation, by my record in other states." One president simply states that "I don't think being Hispanic was an issue."

For the most part, it appears that being Hispanic was neither a major asset nor a major liability on the pathway to the presidency for most Hispanic presidents. As in other presidential selections, fit is important; however, in the case of Hispanics, one's ethnic background does not seem to be a major factor in determining the proper fit. The lessons to be learned by presidential aspirants from Hispanic presidents are similar to the lessons to be learned from other presidents: prepare for the presidency by getting the right degree, the right experience, and the right reputation.

Affirmative Action

Not surprisingly, in light of the above discussion, Hispanic presidents do not view affirmative action as playing a major role in their becoming president. Only one of the ten respondents felt that affirmative action played any role at all. The one who credits affirmative action with playing a role notes that "these programs provided an environment whereby an awareness of the potentials of minority candidates is heightened." Another Hispanic president stated that affirmative action programs did not play a role in his selection. He noted, however, that a "Ph. D. from UC–Berkeley *did* play a role."

Since the major emphasis on affirmative action programs has been directed toward blacks and women, it is likely that the affirmative action programs have not played a major role in the selection of Hispanic presidents and have not placed Hispanics on the national agenda to the extent that women and blacks are on the agenda. Also, if the liabilities of being a Hispanic applicant are no greater than the responding presidents perceive them to be, Hispanics have not felt the need for affirmative actions programs to the degree that women and blacks have.

Mentors and Role Models

Did Hispanic presidents have mentors? Three of the 10 respondents (30 percent stated that they had a mentor who influenced them on their pathway to the presidency. One of the 3 had a president as a mentor; the 2 others had a dean and a school principal.

Eight of the 10 respondents had role models who influenced their careers. Only 1 of the mentors served as a role model also. Four of the 8 presidents had Hispanic role models; 3 of the 4 were the presidents' fathers. Among the other role models were a teacher, a major professor in graduate school, and a public official.

One respondent stated that he had no role model because "there were no other Hispanics in similar or higher positions." While a role model or mentor does not have to be someone in a similar or higher position, the message is nevertheless clear: Hispanic presidents, as is the case with blacks and women, should be sensitive to their potential as role models and mentors, not only for members of their own ethnic group but for others aspiring to the presidency as well.

Negative Role Models

Six of the Hispanic presidents responding to the survey had negative role models. Two of the six role models were presidents, one of whom "disdained students, did not accept women as intellectual peers, was too political, and did not stand for anything." The other negative role model president practiced "reactive leadership, had no trust, was nonsupportive, and was a survivor." One negative "role model" was a vice president for instruction who lacked initiative in addressing the need to change and who had a "complete insensitivity to policy, procedural changes and a leadership style which was not conducive to team management. . . . A 'Moses in the Desert' style of leadership." Another's "inspiration" came from an admissions dean who was "totally incompetent and an embarrassment. He couldn't plan, couldn't make decisions, and possessed terrible interpersonal skills. I'll *never* forget that man."

While the number of negative role models was small, current presidents must nevertheless be sensitive to how they are perceived by others, for presidential actions do indeed speak louder than words. Also, Hispanic presidents, as has been suggested for blacks, women, and all presidents, need to evaluate their obligation to serve as a mentor to those who aspire to the presidency.

Peer Networks

Only one of the Hispanic presidents stated that he was a member of a peer network consisting of Hispanics who aided him in becoming a president. Why do more Hispanics not belong to peer networks? The relatively small number of Hispanic presidents might be one answer. The National Community College Hispanic Council may well be the embryo for such a network; however, as noted earlier, the National Council on Black American Affairs was not listed by black presidents as an effective peer network. Therefore, Hispanics may be well advised to "spin off" an organization similar to the Black Presidents' Round Table. If peer networks are important in the community college profession, then Hispanics should create resources to which potential Hispanic presidents might turn for guidance and professional comradery.

External Contacts

Six of the 10 presidents stated that they had no important external contacts that aided them in becoming presidents. The 4 who listed external contacts as important offered a variety of contacts. One believes that his membership in the Rotary Club was helpful. Another cites the Mexican-American Chamber of Commerce, of which he was president, as being important. Another referred to his community leadership as aiding him in becoming a president. One used his views on education as a way of attracting community attention and ultimately as an aid in his movement to the presidency. His analysis: "I contributed frequent articles to the local and statewide press. I was well known for my stand on the need to raise academic standards. I wrote articles, gave speeches, sat on panels, etc. and was well known for my positions."

As with the blacks, the Chamber of Commerce seems to be relatively unimportant for Hispanic presidents, as are most other "recognized" civic organizations. Sixty-five percent of all current community college presidents belong to the Rotary Club (Vaughan 1986, p. 24) but only one of the 10 Hispanic presidents referred to the Rotary as being important in his career.

Professional Associations

Six of the Hispanic presidents listed professional organizations that aided them in becoming a president. Two cited state organizations as important. Four listed the AACJC and ACE as important. AAHE was listed by one. No one listed the National Community College Hispanic Council. One cryptic response suggests that the support of national organizations is lacking for Hispanics who want to become presidents. His answer to the question regarding help from national organizations: "None, to be brutally frank."

Leadership Programs

Only one of the Hispanic presidents had participated in a program designed to develop leaders. (The survey listed the following programs: ACE Fellows Program; ACE's National Identification Program; and Harvard's IEM, as well as others.) The one who stated that he had participated in programs to develop leaders listed ACE's Institute for Academic Deans.

Do Hispanics suffer from a lack of the attention that has been given to recruiting blacks and women into leadership positions? Or are Hispanics so new and so few in community college leadership circles that they are viewed as not requiring special attention? The answers to these questions are complex and are not provided in the survey responses; however, the questions are worth asking and worth pursuing as more and more Hispanics seek to lead the institutions which enroll so many Hispanic students.

The "Aracial" Presidency?

As with the black presidents, the Hispanic presidents were asked if they viewed the presidency as being "aracial," a term used to describe the ethnic minority Hispanic presidents as well as the racial minority black presidents. Four of the ten presidents do not view the position as aracial. Why not? One states that "we are too visible. The map of Mexico is on our forehead." Another believes that as a Hispanic "you are not expected to succeed. Your actions are always suspect. You must try twice as hard." One Hispanic president believes that "female presidents and Hispanics and perhaps all minorities have to prove themselves early on and repeatedly." He notes, "I have been a CEO for over 12 years at three different institutions, and I must say I have been very successful. Yet people still snicker to my face that I have my position because I am a minority."

In an earlier volume I discussed the "blue-collar presidency," noting that most of today's current community college presidents came from blue-collar homes (Vaughan 1986, 10–15). Certainly moving from a blue-collar background to a college presidency requires that the incumbent bring along certain "baggage" which must be dealt with. One suspects that racial or ethnic minority presidents, the majority of whom also came from blue-collar homes, would not only bring along the baggage of their family backgrounds but also the need to beat the "double standard" by which racial and ethnic minority presidents may be judged. One Hispanic president's comments speak to some of the difficulty in being a minority and a president: "I've always felt that I had to be a better administrator than my non-Hispanic colleagues. I always felt a closer scrutiny by my immediate supervisors. I no longer believe this to be so and have not for some time. I now realize that these pressures were self-imposed."

Only a small number of Hispanic presidents reject the belief that the presidency is aracial. Nevertheless, their remarks suggest that governing boards must guard against applying a double standard in the presidential selection process, for some Hispanics perceive that a double standard exists for them just as it does for women and blacks.

Occupying the Office

Are there advantages to being a Hispanic president? Three of the ten presidential respondents saw some slight advantages in being a Hispanic. From one: "The ability to relate to issues and concerns of the minority population is an advantage." From another: "Students, faculty and community members who are Hispanic tend to support me." He adds, however, that "they really should be a bit more critical and issue-oriented. Prejudice, that is to say, prejudging is wrong regardless of which side it comes from." Another states that "being Hispanic has been an *asset*. Bilinguality and biculturality helps. But being educated at a *major* U.S. institution is a priority." Another speaks to his cultural background. He comments: "My cultural background and my linguistic abilities provide an added dimension of competence. I'm sure my socialization experiences and family ties predispose me to be more tolerant of individual differences and therefore respond to the plight of many of our students."

If cultural ties are important to the successful presidency, most community college presidents should be able to identify with their predominantly blue-collar students. Being able to speak the language of Hispanic students should be an added advantage to community college presidents, especially in those institutions where Hispanic students constitute a large part of the student body. Whether cultural and linguistic ties are enough to compensate for some of the disadvantages associated with being a president from a minority race or ethnic background likely depends upon the situation. In the case of Hispanic presidents, the disadvantages associated with being a minority president appear minor; therefore, in those states with large Hispanic populations, being Hispanic and being able to speak Spanish should be a major advantage to those seeking the presidency. Moreover, one cannot imagine how being bilingual could possibly be a disadvantage for a president under any circumstance.

Chapter

7

THE NEXT
GENERATION

Deans are too dumb to be faculty members and too smart to be
presidents.
—source unknown

It's lonely at the top; It's lonely at the bottom too; But remember, the
top pays more.
—George B. Vaughan

Recently I overheard a dean of instruction[1] at a community college vent-
ing his frustrations over a state-mandated requirement that he provide an
analysis of the issues faced by students transferring to four-year colleges
and universities from his institution. His frustrations resulted not from
the work involved, for he was an indefatigable worker; rather, his frustrations grew out of a statement that he contact his counterparts at the four-
year colleges and universities to which students from the community college transferred. Who, he asked, are "my counterparts"? He pointed out
that the major state university to which most of the students transferred
requires that transfer students be admitted to a specific school or college,
such as the college of arts and sciences or the business school. Schools
and colleges have deans; this university had six who might be viewed by

[1]Dean of instruction is the most commonly used title given to the person who is
responsible for the instructional program at community colleges. Some colleges use the
title academic dean; others, often larger ones, use academic vice president. This chapter
uses the title dean of instruction when referring to the individual in charge of the
college's instructional program.

a state agency as counterparts to the dean of instruction. A quick computation showed that if this dean of instruction followed directions and contacted those who might be viewed by some as his counterparts, he would have to contact approximately thirty-eight individuals at eight universities, a task that would consume more time and energy than he could spare.

An understanding of the role of the dean of instruction, as is true with so much else in the development of the community college, has been gradual and often by trial and error. My wife Peggy, writing about her role as spouse of a dean and president, sheds some light on the evolution of the dean of instruction's position. She relates the story of how I, who in the mid-1960s was about to be appointed dean of instruction at a new community college, caught the president, who was also new in his position, by surprise when I asked him what a dean of instruction does (Peggy Vaughan 1986, p. 171). Peggy did not report the president's answer, but his response to me was "I'll be damned if I know, but if you take the job, we'll find out together." We did find out, but the process was slow and at times difficult.

Anyone familiar with the community college today is not as naive as the new president and I were in the 1960s. Most individuals who work in a community college know in general what the dean of instruction does. Indeed, the above story regarding the request for transfer information tells us something about the role and scope of the dean of instruction's position in a community college, a position that is in some ways unique to these colleges and in other ways quite similar to other positions in higher education.

A volume devoted to a discussion of the role of the academic dean deals entirely with the dean's position as defined at four-year institutions—that is, dean of arts and sciences, dean of engineering. Nevertheless, the book illustrates how the dean of instruction at a community college has a number of things in common with the dean at a university, yet clearly illustrates that the dean of instruction is different from what many conceive a dean to be (Tucker and Bryan 1988). For example, deans of instruction at community colleges perform most of the duties assigned to the chief academic officer at small, four-year private colleges; deans of instruction perform many of the duties performed by provosts or academic vice presidents at major universities; they perform many of the duties performed by the deans of the various schools or colleges within major universities (that is, passing judgment on faculty for tenure and promotions); and many deans of instruction oversee the college's continuing education program, a function performed by deans of continuing education at most colleges and universities with a continuing education division. Deans of instruction even perform some of the functions assigned to deans of professional schools (accreditation and licensure) in those community colleges with nursing and other health programs.

To summarize, deans of instruction deal daily with college-wide issues; pass professional judgment on all teaching faculty; report to and advise the college president; are responsible for the college's programs of study and schedule of classes; help with long-range planning; work with the college's public relations program; plan, monitor, and spend a budget; deal with external agencies; and in general have their fingers on the pulse of the entire college in a way that is equaled only by the college president. The successful dean of instruction must be a leader with vision, a manager of details, an advocate of the faculty, and a representative of the president's office. Indeed, the dean of instruction's position probably requires more time, energy, and attention to a myriad of details than any other administrative position on campus, including that of president. Significantly, the dean of instruction is the only individual on campus who deals with the entire academic program on a day-to-day basis. The dean of instruction has responsibility to ensure that the college does not stray from its central mission of teaching and learning. Ultimately, the effective dean of instruction serves as an "internal auditor" responsible for maintaining the college's academic integrity.

On the other hand, deans of instruction at community colleges do not normally work closely with political leaders, a skill that is required of the successful president. Neither is the dean of instruction expected to have any great depth of knowledge about resource development and fund-raising (Sagaria and Krotseng 1986, p. 3), other activities in which presidents are deeply involved.

Deans of instruction are critical not only to the successful operation of individual colleges but also to the success of the community college in the future, for the dean of instruction is often "only a heartbeat away from the presidency" and is more likely than anyone else on campus to move from his or her position into the presidency. In the pages that follow, an analytical profile of those individuals who will compose the next generation of community college presidents is presented. By knowing who occupies the dean of instruction's position, community college leaders can look into the future and get some indication of who will be leading the nation's community colleges in the year 2000 and beyond, assuming the past is a prologue to future presidential hiring practices.

THE SURVEY

In order to get a glimpse of what the next generation of community college presidents may look like, I asked current deans of instruction essentially the same questions I asked current community college presidents in the survey used to gather data for *The Community College Presidency* (1986).

The survey was sent to 1,169 deans of instruction listed by the American Association of Community and Junior Colleges as serving as their college's chief academic officer; 619 returned the survey, for a response rate of approximately 53 percent. All sections of the country were represented in the responses. The following discussion is based largely on the responses to the survey of deans of instruction. When the deans are compared with current community college presidents, the information on the presidents is taken from *The Community College Presidency,* unless otherwise noted.

Family Background: The Next Generation

In *The Community College Presidency,* I began my study of the presidency by examining the family backgrounds of current occupants of the presidency, including their socioeconomic backgrounds. Accepted indicators of a family's socioeconomic status are the educational level and occupation of the father, assuming the father is head of the household. The educational level and occupation of the mother are also indicators of socioeconomic status. My conclusion, based upon the educational level and occupation of both the father and the mother of community college presidents, was that the community college presidency might accurately be described as the "blue collar presidency" (Vaughan 1986, pp. 10–11). Do the family backgrounds of current deans of instruction mirror the backgrounds of the presidents described in *The Community College Presidency?* Or, are the backgrounds varied enough to conclude that the next generation of community college presidents will be decidedly different from the current generation, at least as far as family background is concerned?

Parents' Education. As reported in *The Community College Presidency,* slightly over 80 percent of the fathers of the presidents surveyed had obtained a high school diploma or less, with 51 percent of them having failed to complete high school. Slightly less than 8 percent had received a bachelor's degree, and less than 8 percent had earned the master's or doctor's degree (ibid., p. 10). The educational background of the mothers of current presidents was similar to that of the fathers and does little to change the image of the blue-collar presidency. Almost 40 percent of the mothers of current presidents had less than a high school education; 38 percent had finished high school; almost 6 percent earned the associate's degree; 10 percent completed the bachelor's; and slightly over 3 percent had the master's or doctor's degrees (ibid., p. 10). The educational background of the fathers and mothers of current presidents clearly demonstrates that community college presidents are socially and economically upwardly mobile, far exceeding both parents in terms of formal education.

The fathers and mothers of the current deans of instruction are somewhat better educated than were the parents of the current presidents. Nevertheless, approximately 75 percent of the fathers and mothers of current deans have earned a high school diploma or less, illustrating that the great majority of deans of instruction come from backgrounds similar to those of the presidents. Interestingly, over twice as many mothers of current deans received the associate's degree as did their fathers, causing one to wonder if the mothers are members of that large group of older adult women returning to the community college.

Parent's Occupations. Among the occupations current presidents listed for their fathers are the following: almost 18 percent of their fathers were employed in administrative-management positions; 14 percent in agriculture; 8 percent in sales; 8 percent in construction; 9 percent in manufacturing and mining; 6 percent in service occupations; and 13 percent in professions (teaching, law, the sciences) that require the bachelor's degree or above (ibid., p. 11). Among their fathers' occupations, current deans of instruction listed the following occupations: 12 percent in administrative-management positions; 14 percent in agriculture; 7 percent in sales; 7 percent in construction; 14 percent in manufacturing and mining; 30 percent in service occupations requiring less than a college degree; and 13 percent in professional fields such as teaching, medicine, law, and the sciences.

Sixty percent of the mothers of current presidents were homemakers. Less than 10 percent were professionals with a bachelor's degree or above (most were educators); and 9 percent were in secretarial or similar positions (ibid.). Forty-eight percent of the mothers of current deans of instruction are homemakers; 10.5 percent are professionals requiring a bachelor's degree or above (most are educators); almost 19 percent are in secretarial or similar work; less than 1 percent are in manager-administrative positions; slightly over 4 percent are nurses or in similar positions requiring at least a two-year degree or diploma from a school of nursing; almost 3 percent are in sales; 8.6 percent work in service occupations; and 4 percent work in manufacturing.

The occupations of both the fathers and mothers of the current deans of instruction indicate that the great majority of deans, just as was true with the great majority of presidents, come from blue collar homes. Just as the presidency was described in *The Community College Presidency* as the "blue collar presidency," current deans of instruction might well constitute the "blue collar deanship." Community college deans of instruction, as is true with current community college presidents, are upwardly mobile individuals who have, in most cases, far exceeded both parents in terms of formal education received and occupational achievements.

Mobility. Forty-five percent of the community college presidents currently serve in positions in the state in which they finished high school. I suggested in *The Community College Presidency* that serving as a president in the state in which one finished high school may be a double-edged sword. Working in a state where one spent one's youth may well provide valuable insights regarding the state's customs, government, schools, and culture that may not be available to an "outsider." On the other hand, working too close to home may encourage one to accept the status quo, be too provincial in outlook, and be too willing to succumb to local political pressures (ibid., p. 15).

An even greater percentage of deans of instruction (49 percent) than presidents (45 percent) are deans in the state in which they finished high school. Female deans are less likely to remain in the state in which they finished high school (40 percent) than are male deans (52 percent); black deans are much more likely to remain in the state in which they finished high school (63 percent) than are either presidents or the deans when viewed as a group; 54 percent of the Hispanic deans live in the state in which they finished high school, a percentage higher than women and deans as a group.

As with the presidents, any conclusions regarding the desirability of staying in the state in which they finished high school would be speculative. The dangers inherent in having two or three generations of presidents and deans from the same general environment could certainly intensify the provincial nature of the community college, raising questions as to how devoted the college is to expanding the mores and attitudes of its students. When governing boards select presidents, they must determine if the "fit" is right for the college and for the individual president. In selecting deans, presidents are faced with the same challenge. However, in addition to determining the right fit, governing boards and presidents have an obligation to select presidents and deans who bring a perspective to the college that will cause students, faculty, and the community to view things differently than they have in the past. Can local and regional deans and presidents bring this new perspective? Obviously, some can and some cannot. In any event, the issue of provincialism is worth considering when employing deans and presidents.

The willingness to move to a new location is one factor that must be considered when seeking to advance in one's professional field. Of the deans responding to the survey, over 67 percent stated that they were likely or very likely to move to a new position within the next five years, although not necessarily to a new state. Ninety percent of those deans who have the presidency as a career goal stated that they are likely or very likely to move into a new position within the next five years, probably a realistic analysis of one of the major considerations one faces when seeking a presidency.

Sex, Race, and Age. A major goal of *The Community College Presidency* was to present a "generic" portrait of those who occupy the position; therefore, the volume did not deal with the sex or the race of the presidents, a shortcoming of the study, I believe. The age of the presidents was included in the study, however. The average age of current college presidents at the time of the study was 50.7 years of age (ibid., p. 209). The average age of current deans is 48.3, an age that is not significantly younger than the average age of presidents, thus dispelling the belief held in some circles that a group of aggressive young leaders waits in the wings for current presidents to retire, move on, die, get fired, or otherwise make way for a "new generation" of leaders. This is true even though those deans aspiring to the presidency are younger (46.2 years old on the average) than the average age of all deans. By most measures, an average age of over 46 years certainly lacks the verve of a "youth movement," especially when one considers that these deans still have to obtain a presidency, a move that the aspiring deans estimate will take approximately four years.

Over 79 percent of the deans of instruction are men, and almost 21 percent are women. While the percentage of female deans is relatively low, it is significantly higher than the 7.6 percent of current presidents of two-year colleges, including private ones, who are women (Green 1988, p. 4). As discussed below, a larger percentage of female deans (61 percent) aspire to the presidency than do male deans (53 percent). The percentage of deans of instruction who are female in relation to the percentage of current presidents who are female indicates that larger percentage of community college presidents in the future will likely be women. The larger percentage of female deans than male deans who aspire to the presidency further indicates that the future will likely see a larger percentage of women occupying the community college presidency.

Presidential Ambitions. Fifty-five percent of the current deans of instruction have the presidency as their career goal. A larger percentage of women deans (61 percent) and Hispanic deans (64 percent) aspire to the presidency than blacks (47 percent) or the deans as a whole.

The average number of years those deans feel will be required to obtain the presidency is 4.0 for all deans; women deans believe that on the average it will require 4.3 years; Hispanics, on the average, believe they will obtain the position in 3.4 years.

Are those deans of instruction who want to become presidents within four years realistic? Perhaps, for a number of reasons. First, the deans have reached a position that many governing boards and community college professionals view as second only to the presidency, and a position which most often serves as the "launching pad" for the presidency. Second, the average number of years (5.4) the deans have been in their current position means that, assuming they obtain the presidency within four years, they will have been, on the average, in the dean's position for over nine years prior to assuming the presidency, a relatively long time in which to demonstrate one's abilities. Third, using 1,059 public community colleges as the base, the average turnover rate for presidents each year from 1984 to 1987 was approximately 127 per year, or approximately 12 percent per year, thereby assuring plenty of "room at the top."[2] Finally, based upon the 333 deans who have the presidency as a career goal and based upon the assumption that the trend will continue whereby approximately one-half of all community college presidential vacancies are filled by deans of instruction (approximately 64 positions per year would be filled by deans of instruction), many of the deans who plan to assume a presidency within four or five years and who have a good chance of ever becoming a president are not being unrealistic in their aspirations. Of course, some deans who aspire to the presidency will never obtain the position.

Pathway to the Presidency. *The Community College Presidency* examined the pathway to the presidency for current presidents. While current presidents came from practically every professional position in the college and a few from outside the community college ranks, clearly the surest way to the presidency is through the academic pipeline. Over 38 percent of the presidents had served as chief academic officers immediately prior to assuming the presidency, and over 7 percent had moved into the presidency from the vice-presidency (Vaughan 1986, pp. 27–28). Of the current female presidents, almost 48 percent were academic deans prior to assuming the presidency, and slightly over 12 percent moved into the presidency from the vice-presidency.

   The Community College Presidency did not examine the presidents' career path beyond asking what position they held immediately prior to assuming the presidency. To determine if the academic pipeline theory held for deans of instructions, deans of instruction were asked what position they had occupied immediately prior to assuming the dean's position. The largest number (29 percent) of the current deans were division chairs immediately prior to becoming dean of instruction. Over 11 percent had been assistant or associate deans of instruction, thus clearly illustrating that the most traveled pathway to the presidency (with the dean of instruction's position being the most important source of presidents) is the academic route: from division chair or assistant dean, to dean of instruction, to president is the road most traveled.

   Just as the academic pipeline is not the only route leading to the presidency (while over 45 percent of the current presidents came from either

---

[2]The following method was used to determine the number of community college presidential vacancies occurring each year in the United States. The year 1985 was chosen as a base year for determining the number of public community colleges in the nation. In that year, the *AACJC Directory* listed 1059 public community colleges. The AACJC directories for the years 1983, 1984, 1985, 1986, and 1987 were examined to determine those presidents who were listed in the directory in a given year but were not listed as presidents for the same institution the following year. For example, if a person was shown as occupying the presidency of a certain institution in 1984 but was not listed as president of the same institution in 1985, the count would show that this college constituted one presidential vacancy for the year 1985.

the dean of instruction's or vice-president's position, 55 percent came from other sources), the assistant dean's or division chair's position is not the only route to the dean of instruction's position. Nine percent of the current academic deans were deans of student services prior to assuming the dean of instruction's position; 9.3 percent were deans or directors of community services; 12.1 percent were faculty members; and over 29 percent came from other positions, including moving from one dean of instruction's position to another. Nevertheless, all of them "trickled up" to the dean's position, and should they now move directly into the presidency, it would be from the dean of instruction's position, regardless of how they reached that position.

Although entering the community college academic pipeline clearly increases one's chances of becoming a community college president, that route is not the only one leading to the office. Nor should it be. By closing the door to more and more "outsiders" such as four-year college deans, public school superintendents, and internal candidates such as deans of community services, deans of student services, and financial deans, the community college may lose much diversity among its leaders, a diversity that is desirable in any healthy organization. In addition, the academic dean should not necessarily be viewed by the board or by the outgoing president as the heir apparent to the presidency. Although approximately 49 percent of the current deans of instruction reached their position through the division chair/vice-president route, the success of 51 percent who chose other routes illustrates that there is no immediate danger of those in the traditional pipeline cornering the market on the presidency, although if one adds the over 11 percent who were faculty members prior to becoming dean of instruction, then the percentage moving through the academic pipeline is increased significantly. Governing boards should be sensitive to the need to bring a number of perspectives to the community college presidency and should work with the faculty to view positions other than that of dean of instruction as a legitimate training ground for the position, although the instructional deanship, all things considered, probably will and should remain the most important single stepping-stone to the presidency.

Academic Preparation. Seventy-six percent of the current community college presidents have the doctoral degree (44 percent have the Ed.D. and 32 percent the Ph.D.); 17 percent of the presidents have master's degrees; the remainder have educational specialist degrees, law degrees, and other degrees and awards. Seventy-seven percent of the presidents with doctorates have them in education, including higher education (ibid., p. 19). How does the educational background of current deans of instruction compare with the current presidents?

Sixty-nine percent of the current deans have doctoral degrees (33 percent the Ph.D., an almost identical figure to the 32 percent of presidents who have the Ph.D., and 36 percent the Ed.D. as compared to 44 percent of the presidents who have the Ed.D.). Sixty percent of the deans with a doctorate have it in education, including higher education; 40 percent have their highest degree in fields other than education. The percentage (60) of the deans with degrees in education is somewhat lower than the percentage (77) of presidents who have the doctorate in education. Somewhat surprising, perhaps, is the fact that 25 percent of the current deans have the master's degree, and a small percentage (slightly over 4 percent) have other degrees, including a few who have only the bachelor's degree.

On the whole, the next generation of presidents coming from the academic deanship will look much like the current presidents as far as academic preparation is concerned.

Professional Associations. The earlier study of the presidency asked the presidents to name the professional organizations to which they belonged, excluding institutional memberships such as the American Association of Community and Junior Colleges. Popular professional organizations for presidents include the Phi Delta Kappa (PDK), with 62 percent of the 410 presidents who belong to a professional organization listing it; the American Association of Higher Education (AAHE), with 53 percent listing it; and the National Association of College and University Business Officers (NACUBO), an organization in which membership is often paid for with institutional dues and which offers multiple individual memberships as a part of institutional membership, listed by 24.6 percent (ibid., pp. 213–15).

Deans of instruction also belong to a number of professional organizations, with 80 percent stating that they belong to at least one. (In considering the following percentages, one should keep in mind that many deans, as is true with many presidents, hold membership in more than one professional organization.) The largest percentage of deans (34 percent) belong to AAHE; 27.5 percent to PDK; 8.5 percent to NACUBO; 6 percent to the Association for the Study of Higher Education; 4.8 percent to the National Association of Student Personnel Administrators (a relatively small percentage when one considers that almost 11 percent of the current deans of instruction were deans of student services prior to assuming their current position and since almost 23 percent of the deans of instruction state that the chief student services officer reports directly to them); 3.4 percent to the American Educational Research Association; 3.1 percent to American College Personnel Association; and over 46 percent to the other professional associations, including discipline-based organizations.

If there are any surprises among the professional memberships of the deans of instruction in relationship to the presidents, they are that such a relatively small percentage of deans (34 percent) belong to the AAHE—one of the most academically oriented major higher education professional association—versus the percentage (over 53 percent) of presidents who belong, and that a relatively small percentage of deans (28 percent) versus presidents (62 percent) belong to PDK. However, the smaller percentage of deans than presidents with doctorates in education would tend to reduce the number of deans joining PDK, since it is an organization for professional educators often promoted by schools of education. It is also possible that invitations to join PDK come after the individual assumes the presidency, implying that the visibility and prestige of the presidency would enhance the possibility of an invitation.

While it is dangerous to generalize about why individuals join professional associations, it nevertheless seems safe to conclude that, based on my own experiences as president and on observations of other presidents at professional meetings, presidents are as inclined to join professional associations for political and social reasons as they are for professional reasons. Therefore, some organizations, and especially the locally based and locally oriented PDK, provide presidents with excellent political and social as well as professional contacts, contacts not as productive or as necessary to deans as to presidents. Other reasons presidents may appear to be more active in some professional associations is that they tend to have more money for travel than other members of the college community; moreover, when presidents travel, someone has to stay at home to "mind the store," and usually that someone is the dean of instruction.

Scholarship. In *The Community College Presidency* it was reported that presidents ranked the ability to produce scholarly publications as having little importance for the president or for those who report to the president, including the dean of instruction (ibid., p. 189). Furthermore, only 39 percent of the presidents indicated that they had conducted research within the last four years and 12 percent stated that they had never conducted research. Thirty-six percent of the presidents stated that they had published something within the past four years and 22 percent reported that they had never published anything (ibid., p. 216).

One would think that if anyone on campus would be devoted to scholarship, it would be the dean of instruction. And how do the current deans fare in their commitment to research and publications? Almost 50 percent state that they have done research within the past five years, and 38 percent report that they have published something within the past five years. By far the most popular form of publication is the article, with 64 percent of those who have published something within the past five years having published an article. Over 8 percent state that they have published a book within the past five years; 4 percent a chapter in a book; 3.5 percent a book review; and 20 percent some other form of publication, including newspaper articles. Although a larger percentage of deans than presidents have done research within the past five years, there is little difference in the rate of publication between presidents (36 percent) and deans (38 percent). Moreover, the time period evaluated for presidents was shorter than that for deans.

Based upon research and publications (a much too narrow interpretation of scholarship for community college professionals), one can conclude that the next generation of presidents as represented by the deans of instruction will tend to mirror the current presidents in these areas. Should scholarship occupy an important place in the professional lives of those deans responsible for the academic integrity of the institution? While one might hope this to be the case, the future does not seem to hold out any great promise in this realm unless the definition of scholarship is broadened and scholarship becomes an important priority for presidents, administrators, and faculty members. One encouraging call for a greater devotion to a broad concept of scholarship in the community colleges comes from the report by the Commission on the Future of Community Colleges. The report states:

> While not every community college faculty member is a publishing researcher, each should be a *dedicated scholar*—including those involved in technical and applied education. But for this to be a realistic goal, the meaning of scholarship must be broadened. In addition to the scholarship of *discovering* knowledge through research, it is also important to recognize the scholarship of *integrating* knowledge, through curriculum development, the scholarship of *applying* knowledge, through service, and, above all, the scholarship of *presenting* knowledge, through effective teaching. (1988, p. 26)

Family and Marital Status. Eighty-seven percent of the deans of instruction report that they are married, whereas 92 percent of the current presidents reported that they were married. Only 1 percent of the presidents reported that they were divorced, whereas 6 percent of the deans of instruction are divorced; 2 percent of the presidents are unmarried (Vaughan 1986, p. 20) and 5.6 percent of the deans are unmarried. Even in marital status, the deans mirror the presidents, although the need to "be married" for the sake of image may be stronger among presidents than among deans, thus accounting for a smaller percentage of single and divorced presidents in relationship to deans.

Sixty-five percent of the presidents reported having children under eighteen living at home, whereas almost 49 percent of the deans reported that they have children under eighteen living at home. Forty percent of the presidents who have children under eighteen living at home; expect at least one child to attend a community college; another 40 percent expect at least one child to attend a public four-year institution; and 11 percent expect at least one child to attend a four-year private institution (ibid.). Almost 29 percent of the deans stated that they expect at least one child to attend a community college; 22 percent a four-year public institution; and 37 percent a four-year private institution.

Seventy-two percent of the presidents and 61 percent of the deans have children over the age of eighteen. Of the presidents with children over eighteen who attended college, 57 percent had at least one child who attend a community college (ibid., pp. 20–23); 32 percent of the deans with children over eighteen have or expect to have at least one child attend a community college. The percentages for public four-year colleges are as follows: 72 percent of the presidents had at least one child to graduate from a public four-year institution (one should keep in mind that many of the same children who attended a community college attended a four-year institution); over 25 percent of the deans have or expect to have a child who will graduate from a four-year public institution; and 9.4 percent of the presidents had a son or daughter who received a degree from a private four-year institution, whereas 43 percent of the deans' children eighteen or older have or expect to receive a degree from a private four-year institution. While the children of deans of instruction appear more likely to attend a private college or university than do the children of presidents, the deans nevertheless view public institutions of higher education, including community colleges, as logical choices for their children.

Activities Beyond the Office. Eighty percent of the presidents belong to one or more civic or fraternal clubs, with almost 65 percent of those stating that they belong to Rotary International; 14 percent belong to the Kiwanis; and 5 percent belong to the Lions Club. Over 11 percent of the presidents stated that they belong to the Masons, a fraternal organization (ibid., pp. 24–25). Sixty-eight percent of the deans of instruction state that they belong to a civic or fraternal organization. While not approaching the 65 percent of the presidents who belong to the Rotary, 26 percent of the deans who belong to a service club belong to the Rotary; 11 percent to the Kiwanis; 8 percent to the Lions; and almost 5 percent to the Masons. As was pointed out by several female deans responding to the dean's survey, the clubs listed on the survey are male-dominated and many, especially until very recently and after the survey was taken, are "male-only" organizations. The fact that there are a larger percentage of female deans than female presidents would account, in part, for the differences in membership between presidents and deans. However, the major reason a smaller percentage of deans than presidents belong to civic organizations is that presidents use civic clubs more than deans to promote the institution and themselves as presidents. As one president from a southern state observed, "Membership in the Rotary Club comes with the presidency in this area."

A smaller percentage of deans (16 percent) belong to a country club than presidents (32 percent), and although 54 percent of the deans use the country club for entertaining, 80 percent of the presidents use it for such purposes (ibid., p. 24). As with membership in civic organizations, country club membership is likely to be more important to presidents in promoting the goals of the college than it is to deans.

Leisure-time activities vary somewhat between presidents and deans. Golf tops the list of sports activities of presidents, with 39 percent of the presidents who engage in sports stating that they play golf. Golf is followed by fishing (34 percent), jogging (31 percent), swimming and tennis (25 percent), skiing (19 percent), and hunting (17 percent) (ibid.). The sports activities of deans of instruction vary, and although they differ somewhat from those of presidents, the difference is in degree and not in kind. For example, jogging (30 percent), not golf (23 percent), tops the list of sports activities for the deans. Twenty-four percent of the deans fish, 14 percent hunt and ski, and 20 percent swim. In no category of sports are the deans more active than the presidents, and a smaller percentage of deans report that they engage in physical activities than do presidents. Any conclusion regarding participation in sports is, at best, speculative. However, some observations regarding sports might shed light on both the deans' and presidents' position.

Presidents may well view sports activities as an extension of the president's office to a greater degree than deans view them as an extension of the dean's office, with many "presidential deals" made on the golf course or tennis courts or while fishing. Or perhaps the explanation lies in the nature of the two positions. While both deans and presidents have their share of stress, the presidency is perceived to be the most stressful position on campus, at least by presidents. If presidents view themselves as constantly under stress, and many do, perhaps they feel that they must do something to combat the situation. The favored way of combating stress by presidents is through physical activity, including participating in the sports listed above (ibid., pp. 127–41). In any event, deans of instruction are physically active and tend to engage in activities that are popular among many Americans.

Spouses. The spouses of deans of instruction have more formal education than the spouses of presidents. For example, 20 percent of the spouses of presidents have a high school diploma or less, whereas 14 percent of the spouses of deans fall into that category; 29 percent of the spouses of presidents have a master's degree, whereas 31 percent of the spouses of deans have a master's degree; 4 percent of the spouses of presidents have the doctorate, compared to close to 9 percent of the deans' spouses who have the doctorate (ibid., pp. 144–47, for information on the spouses of presidents). The spouses of women deans are better educated than the spouses of deans as a whole, with less than 8 percent of them having a high school diploma or less and almost 33 percent having the doctorate.

Over two-thirds of the spouses of community college presidents work in a paid occupation outside the home (ibid., p. 144), whereas over 78 percent of the spouses of deans of instruction work in a paid occupation outside the home. The future will likely see the spouses of community college presidents continuing to work in paid occupations, especially if the percentage of spouses of deans of instruction are any indication. Governing boards should realize this when employing a president and erase from memory any lingering belief that when a president is employed, a nonemployed spouse comes as part of the package.

While there are some minor differences between the spouses of presidents and deans, the differences are not enough to lead one to believe that the future "first family" of the nation's community colleges will be greatly different from the current president-spouse team. To the contrary, the future team will mirror the current one to a large degree.

Hours on the Job. The average reported number of hours worked by deans of instruction is almost 51 hours per week. Female deans work approximately half an hour more per week than do male deans. The great majority of community college presidents report working approximately 50 hours a week, a work load that two-thirds of the presidents consider to be heavy. Presidents earn an average of 21 days of leave annually and take, on the average, 13 days per year (ibid., pp. 212–13). Deans, on the average, earn approximately 20 days of leave annually and take on the average exactly the number of days (13) taken by the president.

Does the president set the standard regarding the number of days of vacation top administrators take? Perhaps. If this is the case, and if two-thirds of the presidents believe their work load is heavy, then presidents should examine the college's leave policies and practices not only for themselves but for the deans of instruction as well.

CONCLUSIONS

The overwhelming conclusion reached here is that the next generation of community college presidents will, assuming the current deans of instruction fill their fair share of the presidencies, be a mirror image of the current generations of presidents in almost all respects. This mirror image runs the gamut, from family background to family life, from academic degrees to views and practices of scholarship, from sports activities to professional memberships. Even the number of days of vacation taken each year by deans is a mirror image of the number of days taken by presidents. As suggested in Chapter 1, there does not seem to be a new breed of leaders waiting in the hallways beyond the community college's open door to assume the presidency and take the community colleges in drastically different directions. If one accepts as fact that many of the next generation of presidents will come from the current group of deans of instruction, then indeed the community college presidency will change little over the next decade, although there will probably be more presidents who are women, blacks, and members of ethnic minority groups such as Hispanics.

If the current deans of instruction are to make up a large portion of the next generation of community college presidents, then governing boards, current presidents, faculty, and anyone else interested in the community college must ask themselves if they are satisfied with the current status of the community college presidency. If the answer is yes, then the nation's community colleges appear to be heading into the twenty-first century in good hands. If the answer is no, then it behooves the powers that be to look at any number of new sources for presidents beyond the community college academic pipeline, including interviewing individuals from outside the community college field such as successful executive officers of business and industry, public school superintendents, and vice presidents and deans from four-year institutions. However, if past practices are precursors of the future, deans of instruction will continue to be in the choice position for assuming the community college presidency.

8

ADVICE FOR THOSE WHO WOULD BE PRESIDENT

For many are called, but few are chosen.
—*Matthew,* 22:14

In addition to the more than three hundred deans of instruction who desire to become community college presidents, many other individuals have the presidency as a career goal. The following advice is based upon my personal judgment and the judgment of others, upon my own experience as a president, and upon my study of the community college presidency.

PREPARATION

The chapter devoted to the deans of instruction offers some clues as to the things one should do to become a president. Similarly, the chapters on women and minority presidents make a number of points that all potential presidents should consider. The following actions and considerations, while in no way guaranteeing anyone a presidency, should aid those who wish to become a president.

Earn a Doctorate. Without the doctor's degree, a candidate's chances of becoming a president will be greatly lessened and indeed eliminated in many cases. One president, when asked about the pathway to the presidency, responded that the "doctorate is, in many cases, the key to the executive washroom. It's considered minimum." In spite of the fact that most presidencies today require the doctorate, some would-be presidents continue to dream that they will be the exception to the rule. For example, in a state with over twenty community colleges and a community college system with a twenty-five-year history during which no one has ever served as a president who did not have the earned doctorate, a dean without the doctorate was deeply hurt because he was not even considered for a recent presidential vacancy. With an increasing number of doctorates granted each year, governing boards do not have to, and few will, consider candidates without the doctorate.

Secure a Position in a Community College. The primary audience for which much of this volume is intended is already "playing in the right game," for approximately 90 percent of the community college presidents come from within the community college ranks, a percentage that has increased over the years and may become even higher in the future. The point is that it is very difficult to obtain a community college presidency from a position outside of the community college field.

Get into the Academic Pipeline. While one can make it to the presidency through routes other than the academic one, the odds of becoming a president increase if the academic path is followed, a point that is emphasized a number of times in this volume and in *The Community College Presidency*. More and more, search committees and governing boards require that presidents possess teaching experience. A successful president of a large community college in the East provides a useful perspective on teaching and the presidency. His advice: "I know that the short cut has been not to bother to teach for many younger presidents. I think that's a mistake. I really would encourage some teaching experience—full time—not just part-time. I think my nine years of teaching before I became a dean were critical to my development." The academic pipeline is from the classroom, to division chair, to dean of instruction, to president.

View the College from a Broad Perspective, Not Just from Your Current Position. Never say "It isn't my problem because I'm only concerned with instructional matters or financial matters or student services." For example, many student services professionals make the mistake of saying over and over that they are "student-oriented." Who isn't? Be college-oriented while at the same time presenting the perspective of your division.

Find a Good Mentor. Edmund J. Gleazer, Jr., former president of the AACJC, offers the following advice:

> Find two or three good mentors. You will find that there are some key people in the field; make it a point to get to know them. Try to get into the

network; go to work for well known and competent people if you can. A good president will employ good people and will provide the opportunity for those people to achieve their own visibility.

While most potential presidents will have difficulty finding even one good mentor, Gleazer's advice is nevertheless sound. If you feel you have outgrown a mentor, find an advocate who has the influence to help you and who is willing to go to bat on your behalf.

Establish a Peer Network. Gleazer's advice that you get into the network is important. Indeed, his concept of mentoring, as outlined above, is more concerned with becoming a part of a professional network than it is with finding a single mentor, although mentoring in the classical sense is important to some individuals. The effective leader establishes and maintains a network of peers who can offer valuable advice, suggest professional opportunities, and serve as professional contacts and references. Community colleges are by definition somewhat provincial; therefore, establishing a peer network requires a great deal of time and energy, but the payoff for those who want to be a president is worth the effort.

Remember, Leadership Begins at Home. Be visible on your own campus. Never miss an opportunity to address the faculty, but be sure you have something worth saying and are well prepared. Serve as the chair of important committees. One of the nation's leading community college presidents places involvement in campus activities at the top of his list of advice for those who want to become a president: "More than anything else, people need to become visible and demonstrate that they are workers and creative and willing to do things. Volunteer to serve on committees, put in extra time, do the extra work without griping about it or asking if you are to be compensated. You will be quickly recognized, and you will be put into the channels to begin to move up." Take stands on important issues, especially those relating to the instructional program. Address the governing board whenever possible, remembering to give plenty of credit to the president. Be friendly with the board, but not familiar. Develop a reputation for getting things done well and on time. Put your name on the reports and papers you produce. You never know when a document will be picked up and quoted both on and off campus, thereby increasing your visibility and reputation.

Never, Ever Base Your Career upon What Someone Else Might Do. While generalizations are dangerous when dealing with anything as complex as moving into the community college presidency, I believe it is safe to say that far too many deans have missed their opportunity to become a president because they have waited around for the current president to leave or retire. People have a nasty habit of not retiring when they say they will. Moreover, most effective deans have made about as many enemies on campus as friends; therefore, it often does not work out that the dean assumes the presidency on his or her own campus.

Become Involved in Community Activities. Pick community activities that will enhance your chances of becoming a president. See the chapter on the mystique of the presidency for a discussion of organizations that might prove helpful.

Be Willing to Move. The majority of presidential vacancies are by definition somewhere else. The person who wants a presidency must be willing to move to a new campus, a new town, a new state. To be "place-bound" often equates to being "career-bound." One successful president who is in his second presidency offers the following advice regarding moving: "If you are not restricted to a certain area of the country, then pick an area where you think there will be growth and go there."

Be Willing to Move to the Hinterlands. Most potential presidents have their Camelot college in mind. They would like to have their first presidency in a place where the quality of life is excellent, the cost of living reasonable, the college high quality, and so on. Rarely is the ideal obtained in the first presidency. A national community college leader offers the following advice: "I think positioning would be the biggest piece of advice I would offer. Position yourself so that you're always in the right place at the right time. I advise some people to take a job though they know they will not stay there for a long time; just position yourself."

A word of caution is in order, however. Do not take a presidency just for the sake of becoming a president. The "fit" should be right for you and the college, and the position, while perhaps not the ultimate one, should be professionally rewarding. Take a position in the hinterlands, do an outstanding job, and make plans to move to Camelot. Incidentally, you will probably find that you like that college in Rural Retreat or Milltown or any number of other locations off the beaten track much better than you think you will, and you will likely stay there much longer than you had expected to stay.

APPLYING FOR THE POSITION:
THE FIRST OFFICIAL ACT

William H. Meardy, former director of the Association of Community College Trustees (ACCT), offers sound advice to presidential applicants. The following appeared in his editorial "A Shot in the Foot: Advice for Presidential Applicants."

> An all too common mistake, made by all too many applicants, is that they either do not know how to, or will not follow directions, as given in the

advertisement. In nearly every ACCT sponsored presidential search advertisement, there appears, IN BOLD PRINT, the following (or words to that effect), "Applicants should state in writing how they meet the following criteria. COMPLIANCE WILL ENHANCE CONSIDERATION." This directive does not say, "A response to the following criteria must be found in the candidate's résumé." It has become apparent to me that many candidates read our request as, "If it is found in my résumé, I don't need to respond." That is not at all what the advertisement requests. Thus the candidate following this line of reasoning has already shot himself or herself in the foot. Other candidates put themselves at an immediate disadvantage with typographical errors, poor grammar, or by leaving some criteria without a response. The lack of a response will necessarily raise questions in the reader's mind. Remember that in most cases, the team of readers have never met you and do not know of your abilities. Therefore, your application must be letter perfect. Almost perfect will not carry the day for you. What board wants to employ a president who cannot follow directions or is sloppy in production? The competition is just too keen to take a chance on an applicant who has already exposed potential flaws.

While keeping Meardy's excellent advice in mind, the following suggestions may further enhance one's chances of being seriously considered for the presidency.

Have Your Letter and Application Typed. It is amazing that someone who is seeking a position with an annual salary of $70,000 or $80,000 will not spend the few dollars it costs to have an application typed, for it is well worth the cost. Make a copy of the application and complete it before completing the original. By completing the copy, you can make sure that the information will fit into the spaces provided. One consultant states: "As simple as it may seem, not developing a 'professional looking' application packet is a common error made by individuals applying for the presidency." While there is no consensus on the topic, you probably should not use your current institution's stationery when applying for a position outside your own institution.

Be Careful about Listing Professional Organizations. List only those organizations to which you *currently* belong. Someone on the board or a member of the college's search committee is likely to belong to that organization you list and to which you have not paid your dues for years. The question you might get about the organization may embarrass you, at the least, and lose you the position, at the worst. Do not list institutional memberships under your own professional membership. For example, membership in the AACJC often shows up on résumés. There is individual membership available for university professors and others, but most memberships are institutional. There are some legitimate crossovers, however. The affiliate councils of the AACJC, NACUBO, and its regional branches and other organizations often offer individual memberships as a part of the institutional membership package.

Sign Your Application and Covering Letter. As elementary as it may seem, individuals sometimes forget to sign their letters of application, an error that in many cases invalidates the application and, in any event, shows a lack of attention to important details. To ensure that you have signed your application, prepare a checklist which includes, among other things, checking for your signature. Also, have someone else review the application for you.

Write the Letter of Application for the Position for Which You Are Applying. A quote from a consultant who has reviewed literally thousands of applications serves to make this point. "I have seen the same letter used to apply for the presidency of a small rural college with an enrollment of under 1,000 and to an urban community college with thousands and thousands of students and very complex dynamics." Another consultant sees a common error as "Sending the same application (no matter how good) to every opening across the country. Develop 'original' applications for each situation." No matter how good the application package is, consultants soon recognize the same package and an "Oh no, not again" syndrome develops. I have seen *exactly* the same package go to four different colleges in one state.

Pay Careful Attention to the "Profile" Developed for the Position. The criteria for positions published in *The Chronicle of Higher Education* and elsewhere should be read carefully, and each point should be addressed specifically. As pointed out rather dramatically in the Meardy quote, today more and more governing boards and college search committees are developing a rather specific list of characteristics and qualifications they are seeking in a president. Some candidates fail to understand that governing boards and consultants put a lot of effort and money into developing the profile for the position and consider it to be very important. To quote a consultant: "It is almost as if some applicants can't read, even though they may possess a Ph.D. degree. The other conclusion would be that there is no concern for the request for information, which is equally as damaging."

Have Someone Check your Grammar. Spelling errors are very common on applications. Search committees tend to be generous with spelling errors, often passing them off as typographical errors. The same is not true of grammatical mistakes, such as subject-verb agreement. Although subject-verb disagreements and other mistakes are less common then "typos," they are more deadly when made. Although community college presidents may not be scholars in the traditional sense of the term, they should be able to write a letter of application that is free from grammatical errors.

Follow the Directions Given on the Application. If the application asks for your academic degrees and requests that you list the last one first, then list the last one first even if your résumé follows a different format. Be clear. A consultant notes that "candidates make it difficult to find dates, e.g., degrees received, where and when; places worked, etc. You have to hunt for these 'nuggets' in a very disorganized résumé."

Meet the Deadline for the Application. You may think, "So I missed the deadline, so what." Unfortunately, you have sent a signal that the position was not that important to you anyway. Late applications also show an insensitivity to the search process, which costs thousands of dollars and consumes many hours of time of a number of individuals. Moreover, although your application is late, it may still be seen by a consultant who will remember seeing it, and when it shows up in a different applicant pool at a later date, the consultant will have a negative image associated with your application. If you cannot make the deadline for a particular position, forget it, for your application will not be considered. Instead of wasting everyone's time, wait until a position comes along in which you are interested enough to make the application deadline.

Fill in All Spaces on the Application. A "not applicable" might be appropriate, but put something in the blank. If your current salary is asked for, give the salary you currently earn and do not project what you will earn next year, even if you are only one month away from a new salary. Do not fudge here, for you are likely to get caught. Even if you are not caught at the moment, you have nevertheless falsified your application, and no one wants to employ someone who lies on an application.

Do Not Leave Gaps in your Employment History Without a Proper Explanation. If you spent two years in the military service, list the two years; if you took three years off to concentrate on raising a family, list the time off and explain what you were doing. If you returned to graduate school, let the search committee know this. Search committees should not be expected to guess what someone did for a couple of years. Indeed, most search committees will not guess; they will simply eliminate an application that is incomplete or confusing.

Either List your Current Supervisor as a Reference or Explain Why You Do Not. The fact that you may view the supervisor as incompetent is not a good-enough reason for not listing the person. Most careful search processes demand that a check be made with one's current supervisor. The reference check of the supervisor may be delayed, upon request, pending your making the "final cut" for the interviews. If you desire that the reference check of the immediate supervisor be delayed, make the request at the time you submit your application.

Do Not Try to Incorporate your Life History into your Letter of Application. If you wish to include a statement of your educational philosophy, do so in an attachment *or as specified* in the directions outlined in the position announcement. If you include a statement on your educational philosophy, be careful and brief. The statement should be well written and grammatically correct. Avoid what one consultant calls "high school–level essays about your philosophy of education." Another consultant warns against including a photograph taken for another purpose. For example, the picture taken for the college yearbook, no matter how attractive, just might not be appropriate for your application some twenty years later. The best advice is not to include a photo unless one is requested.

Do Not Include Irrelevant Material with the Application. Everyone I have ever talked with on the subject of presidential selection—faculty, administrators, board members—resents getting a lot of attachments that are only indirectly (if at all) related to the position applied for. As one consultant notes: "Candidates inundate you with extraneous material, i.e., copies of articles they have written, their district's long range plan . . .," and other material that has little to do with the position at hand.

Give an Indication that you Understand the President's Role. Governing boards and faculty want presidential applicants who not only understand the presidency at the particular college to which they are applying but who also understand it as a professional position with universal characteristics.

Do Not List People Who Hardly Know You as References. Do not make amateurish attempts to use political influence. If you list someone as a reference, make sure the person knows your ability to perform in the position for which you have applied and be reasonably sure your reference will support your candidacy. Do not list more references than requested. (I recall one unsuccessful applicant who listed twenty-one references.) If no set number of references is requested, you should probably list three and never more than five.

Watch the Word Processor. Make sure you include only the name of the college to which you are applying, eliminating all references to the last college to which you sent your letter of application. This advice may sound amusing; however, cases exist where letters of application name one college in one place and another college in another place in the same letter. If you use a form letter, and remember that one of the consultants cited above warns against this practice, make sure you remove the name of the previous college to which you applied.

Do Not Send Too Many "25 Centers." The practice of sending out multiple applications by rationalizing that they only cost the 25 cents spent on a postage stamp is a poor one. That is, be careful about flooding the market with applications for positions in which you have little interest. As is true in being late with your application, word gets around when you casually apply for practically every position that comes along. On the other hand, do not be bashful about applying for positions if you feel they are professionally correct for you. Some deans have been interviewed as many as seven, eight, nine, ten times before obtaining a presidency.

Send the Application to the Person who is Supposed to Receive It. For example, if it is to go to the personnel director or the chair of the search committee, send it to the correct person, *not* to the chairperson of the governing board, even if the chair lives next door. *Do not* send the application to the current president of the college, no matter how well you may know the person, unless you are directed to do so. You are almost guaranteed to turn off the search committee and others by bypassing the established process.

THE INTERVIEW PROCESS: COMMON MISTAKES

Be On Time for the Interview. This is so basic that nothing else needs to be said about it here.

Prepare for the Interview. You should be familiar with the institution to which you apply. Preparing for the interview includes knowing about the college's enrollment, programs of study, composition of faculty and staff, budget, service region, results of recent self-studies, assets, liabilities, and other relevant information. One consultant advises presidential candidates to "Study the auditor's report and don't hesitate to ask penetrating questions" (Weintraub 1987, p. 5). Write the institution for information on the college; write the Chamber of Commerce or similar organizations for information on the area. A good approach is to subscribe to the local newspapers as far in advance of the interview as possible. You should also subscribe to weekly or semiweekly newspapers, if you are applying to a college located in a rural area, and to newspapers that cater primarily to minorities, if such papers exist in the college's service region. Know the names and positions of the trustees in advance, and if possible know the constituency each trustee represents. For example, if you have a black trustee from a black section of the city, you should not be shocked when asked a question related to how the community college should serve blacks. (It may be doing quite well: you should know this, however.) Know the local, state, and national political leaders and their relationship to the college.

Arrive in Town a Day or Two Early. If you are married, the entire family should accompany you, if possible. At the very least, your spouse should accompany you. Check out the cost of housing (you should have obtained information on housing from the Chamber of Commerce; if not, obtain it from a realtor), the reputation of the public schools, and the types and availability of churches, service, social, recreational and cultural organizations. Get a general feeling for the community. You should also take a "straw poll" of the citizens (hotel clerks, waitresses, cabdrivers, realtors, school principals if you inquire about schools, and the "person on the street") to see how the college is viewed by members of the community.

Dress for the Occasion. A male candidate should wear a suit that is in style and suitable for the area in which the college is located. A suit with a western flair might be a big hit in west Texas but will likely lose you the position in Boston or Key West. Shoes are important: boots are out. I recall an incident some years ago when an applicant for a public school superintendency (he was a superintendent at the time he applied but wanted to move to a larger system) was told by the board members that he lost a position in their city because he wore dress boots to the interview. A dean of instruction was eliminated from consideration for a presidency because he wore western boots to the interview. Many governing boards will have a cocktail party and dinner the night before or after the interview. Male candidates should wear a dark suit, a white non–button down shirt, and an appropriate necktie. Female candidates should dress accordingly, keeping accessories unobtrusive and to a minimum. The spouse of the candidate should also dress appropriately.

Wait to Be Asked. Do not assume anything, including taking a seat, until you are invited to do so. Sit up straight; talk plainly and at a level that is appropriate for the room and the situation. Exercise common sense, including good manners.

To Drink or Not to Drink is Not the Question: The Question is What to Drink and How Much. The question of whether to drink alcohol at a board reception is a touchy one. Certainly, if a board has a cocktail party and if the candidate uses alcohol, one drink will do no harm and may help the mood of the evening. On the other hand, neither the candidate nor the spouse should *ever* have enough alcohol during the evening to "feel it." The board may well be in a partying mood; however, neither the candidate nor the spouse of the candidate can afford to be sucked into the party, no matter how much fun the board chair is having. The board will not still love you tomorrow unless your actions are beyond reproach the night before.

On the other hand, the candidate and spouse should drink something (not necessarily alcohol) at the cocktail party, however. Nothing is more disquieting at a cocktail party than to have the guests of honor stand around, arms folded, while others enjoy the drinks. Drinking, or at least holding a glass of mineral water with a twist of lime, occupies the hands and permits the candidate to be a part of the group rather than a by-stander.

Do Not Criticize Your Current President. Word gets around if you do; moreover, criticisms of the person for whom you work may be taken as a sign of disloyalty and even incompetency on your part. If something is wrong at your current college, you should be playing a major role in correcting the problem rather than criticizing the current president.

Do Not Give the Impression That You Are Trying to Leave a Place. Rather than giving the impression that you want to leave your current position, convey the message that you are interested in furthering your professional career by moving into the presidency. State why you are seeking the position. Most colleges do not want a person as president who is running away from his or her current position.

Be Yourself During the Interview, But Do Not Work Too Hard at Being Just "One of the Guys or One of the Gals." Relax some, but not too much. Do not take off your coat or loosen your tie if you are a male, or otherwise make yourself comfortable, no matter what invitation is extended to you by those doing the interviewing. (The invitation to be casual could conceivably be a trap designed to see what you view as proper dress for a president in a formal situation). Do not smoke unless it is a very, very informal situation and unless several others present are smoking.

Be a Good Listener. Respond to the questions you are asked and shut up. For example, if you are asked how you would handle a potential legal problem, give a brief answer; do not respond with briefs on all of the cases dealing with the question at hand. As one well-known former chancellor and present consultant for presidential searches observes: "Too many candidates work at being profound—too profound."

Be Honest. Do not equivocate. If you are caught in a lie, you have probably lost the position. For example, when asked how many people you currently supervise, do not list a number equal to the total faculty. (Moreover, many faculty committees resent the implication that they are being "supervised" by anyone.) If you do not know something, say so and move on. On the other hand, you cannot afford too many "I don't knows," a situation that is unlikely to exist if you prepare for the interview.

Never Talk Down to An Interviewer. This advice is especially true when you talk with the governing board. Remember, you have the primary responsibility to adapt to the interviewer and not vice versa. On the other hand, be subtle in controlling of how the interview progresses. Do not play up to one particular trustee, even if the person is a friend. You may win one vote but lose a dozen. Ideally, the interview should be a conversation with the focus of the conversation on you, the candidate.

If You are Married, Discuss the Role of the Spouse. Does the governing board expect the spouse to entertain at home? If so, are funds and support services available? Is the spouse a professional person in his or her own right? If so, let the board know this during the interview, for some boards still think that when they employ a married president (especially if the president is male), they are getting "two for the price of one," although this belief is not as common today as in the past. Ideally, the spouse should be interviewed by the board if the board has any expectations of the spouse or if the spouse has any expectations of the board.

Ask Questions about Salary, Fringe Benefits, Expectations, Anything and Everything During the Interview. After You have Signed a Contract, It Is Too Late. Discuss your "compromise line," and you must have one. For example, let the governing board know the practices you will use in employing college personnel and that you will not compromise on personnel practices, no matter who recommends whom for employment at the college. However, do not be argumentative during the interview. Make your point as clearly as possible, but do not go to war with the person asking the question, especially over trivial points that have little or nothing to do with how you would function as president. Stated another way, the interview is not the time or place to have a showdown with the chair of the faculty senate, the board chair, or anyone else for that matter. If the salary is unacceptable, say so and tell why. But do not alienate members of the board, for even if your salary demands are met, you may well be off to a bad start with some members of the board.

When considering negotiations during the interview, keep in mind the advice offered by Ruth G. Weintraub, Senior Vice President of the Academy for Educational Development and Director of its Executive Search Division. She cautions: "Don't do any negotiating until you have a clear sense that you are the preferred candidate" (ibid.). That is, do not make too many demands for salary, fringe benefits, and other items that might be negotiable until you have a good idea that you are the one the board is interested in negotiating with.

Be Careful How You Use the Personal Pronoun. You want to give yourself credit for what you have done, but do not appear to take total credit. *No one does it alone.* For example, I recommend that you never refer to "*my* faculty" or "*my* administrators." It is just as easy and certainly more realistic to talk about our faculty or the college's faculty.

Make Sure You are Prepared to Take the Position If It Is Offered, Assuming It is Professionally Right for You and the College. This suggestion does not imply that every position you apply for is the right one for you and should be accepted if offered. But if you reject the position, do it for professional reasons, not because you cannot take the children out of school, sell your house, afford the current mortgage rate, or leave your mother-in-law. You are already aware that these situations represent potential problems; deal with them *before* you apply for a position. Again, word gets around among consultants and board members, so if you drop out of one presidential race because of existing personal reasons, you may be hurt when you apply for future positions. If you are not willing to move unless your spouse can find a suitable position in the new community, state this in your application and during the interview, not *after* the position is offered.

When All Else is Considered . . .

Following the above suggestions will in no way guarantee that you will obtain a community college presidency; however, these suggestions may well help you avoid "shooting yourself in the foot," to use William Meardy's descriptive phrase. By avoiding needless errors, using good judgment in preparing for the presidency, working hard, being in the right place at the right time, and having a bit of luck, you can likely obtain the community college presidency, assuming of course that the interview indicates that the "chemistry," or "fit," is right between you, the college board, the college community, and the community at large.

WHAT TO EXPECT (OTHER THAN THE UNEXPECTED) UPON BECOMING PRESIDENT

A well-known former chancellor of a major community college system sets the stage for this discussion with the following advice:

> As president, expect to work a hell of a lot. Do not go into the presidency because it is going to be prestigious, because you'll have some cards that say president, because you will have a big desk and people will call you president. Go in for the right reasons, and I think the right reasons are commitment, and the belief that your presence is going to make a difference. And you are going to make a difference by working hard, by giving whatever talents you have, and by causing good things to happen. If you plan to go in for other reasons, you shouldn't go in. And if you do you should be kicked out.

A president admonishes those who would be president "to realize that the president's role has changed dramatically from one of an academic role to one of almost a manager of the institution." This advice is especially relevant for those deans of instruction (and other deans) who will be tempted to continue to "play dean" once they become president. Whereas the dean of instruction's position is by definition concerned almost totally with faculty concerns and the instructional program, the president must be concerned with students, staff, the other deans (some of whom may have been viewed as "the enemy" if one assumes the presidency on the campus where he or she is dean), and literally every member of the college community.

Expect to devote what may appear to be an inordinate amount of time and energy to the political process, especially to those political entities that provide funding for the college. Most deans and others who move into the presidency have almost no experience in the political realm; however, if they are to be effective presidents, they must master the process quickly and often with little help, especially in the smaller community colleges.

Another area in which the new president can expect to find frustrations and rewards is in working with the governing board. As is the case with the political process, most individuals new to the presidency have little concept of the time, energy, and skillful planning that goes into the "care and feeding" of the board.

Although the new president can expect to have many of the latest management tools available on demand, this in no way replaces the necessity of dealing with people. Indeed, as society has become more impersonal—as more and more members of the academic community spend more and more time hunched over computers—the presidency requires a better use of interpersonal skills than ever before in the history of the community college. New presidents, as has always been true, must realize that people still need people and act accordingly. Intuition, not computer printouts, may be the most valuable tool a president possesses. At any rate, the successful president must relate well with members of the college community and with external constituents.

The president can expect the governance process to be more complicated at the presidential level than at other levels within the college. If the new presidency is on a unionized campus and the candidate has never worked in a unionized situation, the governance process will take on an important new dimension. The dean of instruction who has spent a career promoting the academic point of view in the governance of the institution must, as president, have a broader view, a view that may conflict with some views held as a dean.

Upon assuming the presidency, one can expect to spend more time not only with political leaders but with other external constituents as well. The external role of the president is very demanding, and there never seems to be enough time to spend with local business and labor leaders, the Chamber of Commerce, or any number of various clubs and organizations that expect the president to join them, work with them, speak to them, or otherwise support them.

Expect to feel pressure to raise funds from private sources. The college foundation is important on most campuses, and the president is expected to provide leadership for the foundation, including calling on potential donors.

The president can expect to deal with pressure groups that, prior to assuming the presidency, he or she did not even know existed. The pressure groups will make demands that are impossible to meet but nevertheless cannot be ignored.

The new president can expect to lose some friends and can expect some feelings of alienation to occur from all segments of the college community. If one assumes the presidency on one's own campus, even old and dear friends on the faculty and staff often become distant. The phrase "lonely at the top" takes on new meaning once the "top" is reached. On the other hand, the president can expect to make new friends, many of whom will be presidential colleagues.

The new president needs to understand the traditions of the institution and work to preserve them. Just as important, perhaps, is the need to establish new traditions, for most community colleges are short on tradition. The traditions must be of a nature that enhances the institution's standing in the academic community and the community at large and must not be viewed as idiosyncrasies of the president.

The president can expect to be called upon to exercise good judgment, to communicate effectively in writing and speaking, to maintain institutional and personal integrity, to act and think courageously, and to exercise other accepted characteristics of good leadership that have been around for thousands of years.

Finally, as a community college president, you can expect to occupy the most exciting position on campus and perhaps in all of higher education. As one president describes the presidency, "When it is good, it is very, very good."

BIBLIOGRAPHY

Baldridge, J. V. *Power and Conflict in the University*. New York: Wiley, 1971.

Benezet, Louis T. "Do Presidents Make a Difference?" *Educational Record* 63, no. 4 (Fall 1982): 11–13.

————, Joseph Katz, and Frances W. Magnussion. *Style and Substance: Leadership and the College Presidency*. Washington, DC: American Council on Education, 1981.

Blocker, Clyde E.; Plummer, Robert H.; and Richardson, Richard C., Jr. *The Two-Year College: A Social Synthesis*. Englewood Cliffs, NJ: Prentice-Hall, 1965.

Bok, Derek. *Higher Learning*. Cambridge, MA: Harvard University Press, 1986.

Boyer, Ernest L. *College: The Undergraduate Experience in America*. New York: Harper and Row, 1987.

Burns, James MacGregor. *Leadership*. New York: Harper and Row, 1978.

Clodius, Joan E., and Magrath, Diane S., eds. *The President's Spouse: Volunteer or Volunteered*. Washington, DC: National Association of State Universities and Land-Grant Colleges, 1984.

Cohen, Michael D., and March, James G. *Leadership and Ambiguity: The American College President*. New York: McGraw-Hill, 1974.

Commission on the Future of Community Colleges. *Building Communities: A Vision for a New Century*. Washington, DC: American Association of Community and Junior Colleges, 1988.

Cyert, Richard M. "Managing Universities in the '80s," in Chris Argyris and Richard Cyert, *Leadership in the '80s: Essays on Higher Education*. Cambridge, MA: Institute for Educational Management, Harvard University, 1980.

Deegan, William L., Dale Tillery, and Associates. *Renewing the American Community College*. San Francisco: Jossey-Bass, 1985.

DeLoughry, Thomas J. "Students Shut Down University for the Deaf, Force Newly Named President to Resign." *Chronicle of Higher Education*, March 16, 1988: A1–A18.

Dodds, Harold W. *The Academic President: Educator or Caretaker?* New York: McGraw-Hill, 1962.

Ehrhart, Julie Kuhn, and Sandler, Bernice R. "Looking for More than a Few Good Women in Traditionally Male Fields." Project on the Status and Education of Women, Washington, DC: Association of American Colleges, 1987.

Fisher, James L. *The Power of the Presidency*. New York: American Council on Education/Macmillan, 1984.

Gardner, John W. *Attributes and Context*. Leadership Papers, no. 6. Washington, DC: Independent Sector, April 1987.

Gardner, John W. *The Tasks of Leadership*. Leadership Papers, no. 2. Washington, DC: Independent Sector, March 1986.

Gardner, John W. *The Heart of the Matter*. Leadership Papers, no. 3. Washington, DC: Independent Sector, June 1986.

Green, Madeleine F. *The American College President: A Contemporary Profile*. Washington, DC: American Council on Education, 1988.

Harvey, William B. "An Ebony View of the Ivory Tower: Memories of a Black Faculty Member." *Change: The Magazine of Higher Learning* vol. 19 (May/June 1987): 46–49.

Hofstadter, Richard. *The Age of Reform: From Bryan to F.D.R.* New York: Vintage, 1955.

Jencks, Christopher, and Riesman, David. *The Academic Revolution*. Garden City: Doubleday, 1968.

Kauffman, Joseph F. *At the Pleasure of the Board: The Service of the College and University President*. Washington, DC: American Council on Education, 1980.

Keller, George. *Academic Strategy: The Management Revolution in American Higher Education*. Baltimore: Johns Hopkins University Press, 1983.

Kerr, Clark. "Foreword." In Frederick Rudolph, *Curriculum: A History of the American Undergraduate Course of Study Since 1636*. San Francisco: Jossey-Bass, 1977.

Kerr, Clark. *Presidents Make a Difference*. Washington, DC: Association of Governing Boards of Universities and Colleges, 1984.

Kerr, Clark, and Gade, Marian L. *The Many Lives of Academic Presidents*. Washington, DC: Association of Governing Boards of Universities and Colleges, 1986.

Maccoby, Michael. *The Gamesman: The New Corporate Leaders*. New York: Simon and Schuster, 1976.

"Marilyn Schlack." *Encore: Magazine of the Arts, September–October 1987:* 6–25.

Martin, Warren Bryan. *A College of Character*. San Francisco: Jossey-Bass, 1982.

Meardy, William H. "A Shot in the Foot: Advice for Presidential Applicants." *ACCT Advisor* vol. 18 (March 1987): p. 2.

Pullias, Earl V., and Wilbur, Leslie. *Principles and Values for College and University Administration*. New York: Philosophical Library, 1984.

Sagaria, Mary Ann, and Krotseng, Marsha V. "Deans' Managerial Skills: What They Need and What They Bring to the Job." *The Journal of the College and University Personnel Association* vol. 37 (Summer 1986): 1–7.

Shavlik, Donna, and Touchton. Judith G. "Women as Leaders." In *Leaders for a New Era: Strategies for Higher Education*, edited by Madeleine F. Green. New York: American Council on Education/Macmillan, 1988.

Stoke, Harold W. *The American College President*. New York: Harper and Brothers, 1959.

Tucker, Allan, and Bryan. Robert A. *The Academic Dean: Dove, Dragon, and Diplomat*. New York: American Council on Education/Macmillan, 1988.

Vaughan, George B. *The Community College Presidency*. New York: American Council on Education/Macmillan, 1986.

Vaughan, George B. *Balancing the Presidential Seesaw*. Charlottesville: Southern Association of Community and Junior Colleges, Occasional Paper no. 2, vol. 4 (July, 1986).

Vaughan, George B. "Scholarship in Community Colleges: The Path to Respect." *Educational Record* vol. 69 (Spring 1988): 26–31.

Vaughan, George B., and Associates. *The Presidential Team: Perspectives on the Role of the Spouse of a Community College Presidents*. Washington, DC: American Association of Community and Junior Colleges, 1987.

Vaughan, Peggy A. "Being There: One Spouse's Perspective." In George B. Vaughan, *The Community College Presidency*. New York: American Council on Education/Macmillan, 1986.

Weintraub, Ruth G. 1987. "Ten Caveats for Presidential Candidates." *Academy News* vol. 10 (May 1987.): p. 5.

Wilson, Reginald, and Melendez, Sarah E. "Strategies for Developing Minority Leadership." In *Leaders for a New Era: Strategies for Higher Education*, edited by Madeleine F. Green. New York: American Council on Education/Macmillan, 1988.

INDEX

Academic deans. *See* Deans of instruction
Academic leadership, 21, 27
Academic President: Educator or Caretaker? (Dodds), 19
Academic Revolution, The (Jencks and Riesman), 30
Affirmative action, 67
  black presidents and, 91, 93–94
  female presidents and, 78–80
  Hispanic presidents and, 104
Age of Reform, The (Hofstadter), 31
Alcohol, 134–135
Aloofness, 33
Alverno College, 31
American Association of Community and Junior Colleges (AACJC), 1*n*, 66, 82, 96, 106, 111, 116*n*, 118, 129
American Association of Higher Education (AAHE), 82–83, 96, 106, 118
American Association of University Professors (AAUP), 96
American Association of University Women, 83
American Association of Women in Community and Junior Colleges, 66, 82
American College Personnel Association, 118
American College President, The (Stokes), 23
American Council on Education (ACE)
  Fellows Program, 83, 97, 106
  Institute for Academic Deans, 106
  National Identification Program, 83, 106
American Educational Research Association (AERA), 118
Application, 129–133
Aracial presidency, 97–99, 106–107
Asexual presidency, 83–85
Association for the Study of Higher Education, 118
Association of Community College Trustees, 62
Association of Governing Boards of Universities and Colleges, 30, 48, 62
Atlas, Charles, 13

"Balancing the Presidential Seesaw" (Vaughan), 11*n*
Baldridge, J. Victor, 14, 30

Benezet, Louis T., 30, 40
Black community college presidents, 65–68, 87–101
  advantages of, 99–101
  affirmative action and, 91, 93–94
  aracial presidency issue, 97–99
  assets and liabilities of candidates, 90–92
  interview, 89–90
  leadership programs and, 96–97
  mentors and role models and, 94–95
  negative role models and, 95
  pathway to presidency, 88–90
  peer networks and, 95
  professional associations and, 96
Black Presidents' Round Table, 95, 96, 105
Black underground, 96
Blocker, Clyde E., 4*n*
Bogue, Jesse, 6
Bok, Derek, 31
Boorstin, Daniel, 32
Boyer, Ernest, 26, 31
Bryan, Robert A., 110
Bryn Mawr College, HERS program of, 83
Burnout, 46*n*
Burns, James MacGregor, 33

Campus climate, 8, 10–11, 14, 21, 57
Carnegie Foundation, 96
Chamber of Commerce, 82, 85, 96, 106
Charismatic power, 38
Chemistry, 58–59, 77, 90, 92, 137
Chronicle of Higher Education, The, 130
Clark, Burton, 60
Clodius, Joan E., 48
Coalitions, shifting, 14–15
Cohen, Michael D., 30, 59–60
Commission on the Future of Community Colleges, 120
Community activities, 37, 41, 42, 128, 138–139
Community College, The (Bogue), 6
Community college presidency. *See also* Deans of instruction
  advice for applicants, 125–137
  background of, 34–37
  bringing focus to, 8–11
  campus climate creation, 8, 10–11, 14, 21, 57

143

Community college presidency
(*continued*).
    educational leadership and. *See* Educational leadership
    females and. *See* Female community college presidents
    founding presidents, 1–7, 23, 34–37
    hours worked, 123
    leisure-time activities, 122–123
    management function, 8, 9–10, 14, 21
    metaphor for, 11–16
    minority presidents. *See* Black community college presidents; Hispanic community college presidents
    mission communication, 8, 11, 14, 15, 21
    mystique of. *See* Mystique of community college presidency
    shifting focus of, 6–8
    tenure, 28, 35, 46–63
Community College Presidency, The (Vaughan), 46*n*, 111–113, 116, 119, 126
Commuter marriages, 74
Cooling-out hypothesis, 59–60
Council on Black American Affairs, 96
Creative tension, 13
Critical review, 26
Curriculum development, 18
Curriculum reform, 19–22, 31
Cyert, Richard M., 17, 22

Danforth Foundation, 96
Deans of instruction, 109–123, 138
    academic preparation, 117–118
    age and gender of, 115
    family and marital status of, 120–121
    family background of, 112–113
    hours worked, 123
    leisure-time activities, 122–123
    mobility and, 113–114
    pathway to presidency, 116–117
    presidential ambitions, 115–116
    professional associations and, 118–119
    scholarship and, 119–120
Declaration of Independence, 87
Deegan, William L., 8
Defensiveness, 51–52
Delegation, 40–41
DeLoughry, Thomas J., 77
Distance, 38–40
Dodds, Harold W., 17, 19
Double standard, 67, 72, 76, 97
Douglas, Kirk, 32
Dress, 134, 135
Dynamic tension, 13–14

Educational leadership, 17–31
    as focus for presidency, 21–23
    in perspective, 30–31
    prerequisites to, 23–27
    scholarship and, 24–30

Educational philosophy, 23, 131–132
Ehrhart, Julie Kuhn, 76
Elion, Gertrude B., 65
Enrollment, 1*n*, 6

Female community college presidents, 65–86
    advantages and disadvantages of, 85–86
    affirmative action and, 78–80
    asexual presidency issue, 83–85
    assets and liabilities of candidates, 72–78
    interview, 71–72
    leadership programs and, 83
    mentors and role models and, 80
    negative role models and, 80–81
    pathway to presidency, 69–72
    peer networks and, 81–82
    professional associations and, 82–83
Fisher, James, 30, 36, 38, 39, 48, 62
Founding community college presidents, 1–7, 23, 34–37
Friday, William, 30

Gade, Marian, 30, 37, 83, 97
Gallaudet University, 77
Gamesman concept, 5–6, 8
Gardner, John W., 3, 4, 6, 39
Gleazer, Edmund J., Jr., 2, 4*n*, 126–127
Graduation ceremonies, 35
Grammatical errors, 130
Grant, Cary, 32
Green, Madeleine F., 65
Green, Robert L., 32

Harvard University, Institute for Educational Management of, 83, 96, 106
Harvey, William B., 101
Henderson, James C., 46
Hesburgh, Theodore M., 30
Hispanic community college presidents, 65–68, 101–108
    advantages of, 107–108
    affirmative action and, 104
    aracial presidency issue, 106–107
    assets and liabilities of candidates, 103–104
    interview, 102
    leadership programs and, 106
    mentors and role models and, 104
    negative role models and, 105
    pathway to presidency, 101–102
    peer networks and, 105
    professional associations and, 106
Hofstadter, Richard, 31
Hot line, 62

Inauguration ceremonies, 36, 45
Institution management, 8, 9–10, 14

Interview
  black presidents and, 89–90
  common mistakes, 133–136
  female presidents and, 71–72
  Hispanic presidents and, 102
Introspection, 62
Intuition, 138
Issues analysis, 26

Jefferson, Thomas, 4
Jencks, Christopher, 30, 36

Katz, Joseph, 40
Kauffman, Joseph, 9
Keller, George, 9
Kent State University, 30
Kerr, Clark, 20, 24, 30, 37, 46, 48, 83, 97
Kiwanis Club, 121
Krotseng, Marsha V., 111

Leadership and Ambiguity (Cohen and
    March), 30
Leadership by example, 27–28
Leadership programs
  black presidents and, 96–97
  female presidents and, 83
  Hispanic presidents and, 106
Legitimate power, 36
Leisure-time activities, 122–123
Lions Club, 121
Low-energy, high-yield activities, 43

Maccoby, Michael, 5, 8
McKnight Black Doctoral Fellowship
    Program, 96–97
McMurty, Larry, 1
Madison, James, 4
Magnusson, Frances W., 40
Magrath, Diane S., 48
Management function, 8, 9–10, 14, 21
"Management Time: Who's Got the
    Monkey?" (Onchen and Wass), 44n
*Many Lives of Academic Presidents,
    The: Time, Place, and Character*
    (Kerr and Gade), 30, 83
March, James G., 30, 59–60
Martin, Warren, Bryan, 27
Masons, 121
Massey, Walter E., 65
Meardy, William H., 128–130, 137
Media, 42–43
Meléndez, Sarah E., 93, 95, 97, 100
Mentors, 67, 126–127
  black presidents and, 94–95
  female presidents and, 80
  Hispanic presidents and, 104
Mexican-American Chamber of Com-
    merce, 105
Miami-Dade Community College, 31
Midcareer crisis, 8

Minority presidents. *See* Black commu-
    nity college presidents; Hispanic
    community college presidents
Mission communication, 8, 11, 14, 15, 21
Motherhood, female presidents and, 71
Mystique of community college presi-
    dency, 32–45
  background of presidency and, 34–37
  delegation and, 40–41
  distance and, 38–40
  enhancement of, 42–45
  need for, 33–34

National Association for the Advance-
    ment of Colored People, 96
National Association of College and Uni-
    versity Business Officers
    (NACUBO), 96, 118, 129
National Association of Student Person-
    nel Administrators, 118
National Community College Hispanic
    Council, 66, 105, 106
National Council of Black American Af-
    fairs, 66, 95, 105
Negative role models, 67
  black presidents and, 95
  female presidents and, 80–81
  Hispanic presidents and, 105
No confidence vote, 57–58, 61
Northeast Missouri State University, 31

Old boys' network, 67, 70–71, 82, 90, 95
Old girls' network, 82
Onchen, William, Jr., 44n
Ownership syndrome, 51

Participatory governance, 38, 39
Peer networks, 127
  black presidents and, 95
  female presidents and, 81–82
  Hispanic presidents and, 105
Phi Delta Kappa (PDK), 96, 118–119
Philosophy of education, 23, 131–132
Plummer, Robert H., 4n
Political process, 138
Power of the Presidency, The (Fisher),
    30, 38
Pragmatism, 25, 29, 32
Presidency. *See* Community college pres-
    idency
Presidential applicants, advice for,
    125–137
Presidential hot line, 62
Presidential platform, concept of, 38, 39
Pressure groups, 37, 139
Pride in community colleges, 29–30
Professional associations, 129
  black presidents and, 96
  deans of instruction and, 118–119
  female presidents and, 82–83
  Hispanic presidents and, 106

Professional meetings, 28
Professional renewal, 29
Promotion, 28
Provincialism, 29
Publication, 27, 28, 119
Pullias, Earl V., 10

References, 131, 132
Research, 26, 119
Resource allocation, 9
Résumes, 129–131
Reverse delegation, 44
Rewards system, 28
Richardson, Richard C., Jr., 4n
Riesman, David, 24, 30, 36, 38, 39, 48
Risk-taking, 59
Rockefeller Foundation, 96
Role models, 67
   black presidents and, 94
   female presidents and, 80
   Hispanic presidents and, 104
Rotary Club, 43, 84, 86, 105, 106, 121

Sabbaticals, 29, 62
Sagaria, Mary Ann, 111
Sandler, Berenice R., 76
Schlack, Larry, 74
Schlack, Marilyn, 74
Scholarship, 62
   commitment to, 24–27
   deans of instruction and, 119–120
   defined, 24–25
   educational leadership and, 24–30
   forums devoted to, 28–29
   rewards system and, 28
"Scholarship in Community College: The
   Path to Respect" (Vaughan), 24n
Seesaw metaphor, 12–16, 60
Self-confidence, perceived, 38, 62
Sexism, 84
Shavlik, Donna L., 70, 75, 76, 79
Shifting coalitions, 14

Socrates, 62
Spouses
   of deans of instruction, 122–123
   of presidents, 5, 6, 62, 68, 72, 74, 136
Stereotyping, 67, 70
Stokes, Harold W., 23, 25
Student assessment, 19–20, 22
Style, 38

Tenure of community college presidents,
   28, 35, 46–63
Tillery, Dale, 8
Touchton, Judith G., 70, 75, 76, 79
Truman, Harry S., 1
Trustees, 43–44, 47, 57–60, 62, 76, 77,
   133, 134, 138
Tucker, Allan, 110
Two-Year College, The: A Social Synthe-
   sis (Blocker, Richardson, and Plum-
   mer), 4n

Unions, 37, 138
United Way, 85
University of Central Florida, 69
University of Texas, Austin, 96
Urban League, 96
Uses of the University, The (Kerr), 30

Vacations, 29, 123
Vaughan, George B., 2, 6, 11, 17, 21,
   24n, 27, 29, 35, 38, 47, 48, 61, 72,
   73, 82, 84n, 87, 96, 106, 107, 109,
   120
Vaughan, Peggy A., 1, 110

Wass, Donald L., 44n
Weintraub, Ruth G., 133, 136
Wilbur, Leslie, 10
Wilson, Reginald, 93, 95, 97, 100

Young Mens' Christian Association
   (YMCA), 96